RUNNING FREE

RUNNING FREE

An *Incredible Story* of *Love*, *Survival*,
and *How 200 Horses* Trapped in a Wildfire
Helped *One Woman* Find Her *Soul*

AMI CULLEN

Running Free

An Incredible Story of Love, Survival, and How 200 Horses Trapped in a Wildfire Helped One Woman Find Her Soul

Ami Cullen

ISBN 979-8-218-47214-6
Published by www.RunningFreeHorses.com

Celebrated for over a century for its rustic elegance, legendary service, and exceptional horsemanship, The C Lazy U guest ranch in Granby, Colorado, found itself in the destructive path of one of the worst fires in the recorded history of Colorado—the East Troublesome Fire—in October 2020. *Running Free* is a fictionalized account of this event.

This book is dedicated to C Lazy U employees who worked selflessly for countless hours to save the ranch and the horses, as well as the Colorado Equine Community, who came together to volunteer their time and resources to save over two hundred horses. Heartful thanks also go to the Grand County firefighters who went over and above the call of duty to save the C Lazy U.

CONTENTS

CHAPTER 1

TROUBLE

OCTOBER 14, 2020

9:00 AM

The East Troublesome Fire.

Troublesome, as if the fire was like some troublesome toddler who throws tantrums at Safeway or always wants just one more drink of water or knocks that drink of water over in the restaurant.

I know. The name of the fire is not surprising, considering its origin occurred east of Troublesome Creek in the Arapaho National Forest. And I know that wildfires are part of the agreement when you move out West. So, by nature of that fact, they are going to be troublesome. But geez, it felt like the whole state of Colorado was on fire that summer. Regardless, the other fires never directly affected us, so I don't think we had any idea how troublesome the fire would become as the second-largest and fastest-moving fire in Colorado's recorded history, threatening countless people and their homes, as well as the lives of hundreds of horses.

October 14 began like most days on the ranch. I could hear Lexi singing the chorus of a Keith Urban song as she tacked up the horses with the other wranglers for the morning trail ride. The sound of omelets sizzling on Chef Antonio's cast iron skillet filled the air as the guests emerged from their luxury cabins in a trickle, lured to the lodge by that cowboy coffee-and-campfire, bacon-and-eggs smell that is somehow always better in the clear Rocky Mountain air—especially that late into the season. That fall had been so warm and dry that everyone was carrying their plates outside to the patio to enjoy Antonio's culinary delights. Tom gave me a peck on the cheek as I gave a quick nod to the family of four walking through the door of the lodge. Then I made my way to the corrals to prepare for a full day of guest activities.

The parents looked as if they had spent the night before either drinking heavily, arguing relentlessly, or unsuccessfully trying to put the kids to bed—or a combination of the three. The wife's makeup couldn't hide her dark circles, and it was clear that her investment banker husband's scruff of a beard was not his norm. But hey, we're on a dude ranch, right?

The children, in contrast, had bottled up everyone's energy from the cabin and let it spring forth as they burst through the door and raced over to give Nicole a hug.

Nicole, the children's head camp counselor at C Lazy U Ranch, cheerfully hugged the children back, adeptly redirecting them to their parents and reminding them it was time for breakfast.

"Time to eat up so you're ready for more riding!" she said.

Brother and sister high-fived and raced back to their parents, begging for French toast and locally cured ranch bacon, *right now, please!*

That's when the radio call came in.

"Emme, it's Jack," Molly said, extending her portable two-way radio toward me.

I rolled my eyes. *Really? Jack's calling already, and the day has barely begun. It's probably the Radshaws again, requesting another private riding lesson for their daughter. Or an additional spa treatment. Or a private wine tasting with Steven.*

Before I clicked over to channel two, Molly added, "Sounds urgent."

My annoyance was replaced by a sensation I knew all too well: it was what I call *that feeling*. It was a feeling in the pit of my stomach—my gut—where I just knew something was wrong. It's the same place I had *that feeling* the day I stepped into Krinsky and Sheirburg for the first time. The same feeling I got the day I came home to Reed for the hundredth (no, millionth) time and surveyed the dimly lit penthouse, with the empty wine bottles and the monotonous hum of *Grand Theft Auto* in the background.

Thank God, sometimes *that feeling* lets me know something is *right*. Like the day I met Tom. Or flew out to C Lazy U with Laura in 2007. Or mounted a horse as a six-year-old for the very first time.

But on October 14, *that feeling* wasn't the good kind. I turned the dial to channel two and put it to my ear. *Why is Jack calling now?* I wondered as I said, "Hello?"

"Emme?" came the voice of the ranch's general manager, Jack Olsen.

"Hey, Jack. What's up?"

"Um, we've got a potential problem. Did you see that wildfire everyone is talking about on Facebook?"

"Mm-hmm . . . ?" My voice trailed off, as I already sensed what he would say next.

"Well, we're not entirely clear what's happening. And it's difficult to predict, since the fire is past Elk Mountain, some fifteen miles away as the crow flies. But everyone's buzzing about what would happen if the fire *were* to make its way here."

"Do they really think it's going to come our way? I thought it was just a small brush fire." I gripped the radio even more tightly.

"Right now, I'm basing a lot of this off what I'm seeing on Facebook. So, who knows how accurate this is—which is why I don't want to panic. However, I was thinking about all the beetle-kill trees littering the forest floor. Even the smallest spark from a hunter's shotgun could spell disaster." Jack paused. "Hey, do you have access to Russell's files to see if there is some protocol about moving the horses we should know about? Just in case?"

I mentally combed through the files Russell left me when he retired. "I don't remember the specifics, but I'm almost positive he had a set of plans. I'll take a look."

"Sounds good. Oh, and Emme. Please remember, we're not in imminent danger. We just need to keep an eye on things."

I chuckled to myself, appreciating Jack's attempt to downplay his call. *Even Jack knows how neurotic I can get over the smallest things.*

After clicking the radio off, I did my best to push the disturbing feelings aside and reminded myself that maybe I was only being paranoid. I mean, I do tend to overreact at times.

C'mon, Emme. Relax. The fire is well over fifteen miles away! And Jack said the chances are really slim that we would ever be in its path. So, how bad could it possibly get?

4:30 PM

This time, when Molly handed me the radio, I hesitated. The feeling had returned, even stronger this time, as I answered.

"Hey, Jack. What's up?"

He cleared his throat. "Well, I still think the fire chief may be overreacting, but now he's telling me to prepare for the worst-case scenario. Apparently, the fire is now close to four thousand acres and burning fast."

My stomach tightened. "What would a worst-case scenario look like?"

"It means they would put us into pre-evacuation, where we would need to get everyone off the ranch."

"Everyone . . . as in the horses?"

"That's exactly what I mean. People, horses, donkeys, you name it. But look, let's not panic . . . at least not yet. Remember that the fire chief needs to think about the worst things that can possibly happen—even if they don't. But the fire *is* moving fast, and God forbid it jumps to this side of Elk Mountain. With all that fallen dead timber between here and there, that area is, quite frankly, a tinderbox."

"Yeah, I know." I looked out the window. "And is it my imagination, or does the sky look even smokier than it was a few hours ago?"

"Unfortunately, it's not your imagination. The chief mentioned the smoke to me too. Obviously, none of this is good for anyone's lungs—including the horses'."

"So what do we do next?"

"At this point, I think you should alert the wranglers that we may need to cancel rides tomorrow if things get worse through the night. But please, Emme, without panicking anyone. I'm still trying to be optimistic."

"Got it."

I clicked off the radio and sank into my office chair, wondering how I was going to tell them without either putting them over the edge or downplaying it so much that they didn't even care.

Man, I wish Russell were still here to help. He would know what to do.

BCLU

SUMMER 2007

I like to call my days before I became a wrangler (the one in charge of the horses)—and later the ranch's head wrangler—my "BCLU" days: before C Lazy U.

I know, I know. It sounds like BC and AD eras from history class. Of course, I'm not so vain as to think of my life like before Christ, but the difference between my years working for C Lazy U and the years that preceded this chapter of my life might appear to be stories about two dramatically different people: East Coast lawyer Emme versus Western Emme. Hunter/jumper society versus dude ranch life.

So, how did a Philly lawyer become a Colorado cowgirl, one may ask?

Maybe it was the jingle or the trail rides or the amazing friendships I made on the ranch. Or just the sheer magic that seems to exist at C Lazy U. One thing I do know is that the I-need-to-be-here-forever feeling started to work its way into my consciousness my first day on the ranch—watching the jingle as a guest.

The first time I saw the jingle, on vacation in 2007, I couldn't believe what I was seeing and absolutely knew I wanted to be a part of it. The wranglers leading two hundred horses from pasture to the corrals is one of the most breathtaking sights in the world. You can literally feel the thunder from the horses' feet as they're running together, synchronized, toward the same location and the wranglers are keeping everything *mostly* in perfect order. This daily ritual on the ranch never fails to instill a sense of awe in the guests. In fact, witnessing the jingle for the first time brings most to tears.

That first time, as the ground shook beneath my feet and the horses galloped past Laura and me, I couldn't breathe. Something in my solar plexus opened, as if a gaping hole that I didn't even know existed might finally have been filled. I knew instantly that I never wanted to leave this place.

But the excitement didn't stop there, because Laura and I had a full week of riding ahead of us. We had even signed up for a full-day excursion: an all-day trail ride on Gold Run.

As we waited for the group to assemble for the ride, Laura and I were giddy with excitement. I remember sticking my sweaty, shaking hands in the pocket of my Wranglers, taking a deep breath, and attempting to hold my posture in a relaxed yet confident way. I sat on my assigned horse,

Gunsmoke, for the week, as if to say, "Hey, I do this every day. No big deal."

Even though riding and horses have always felt like home to me, something about riding here, at the ranch, felt different from the stifling, controlled environment in the hunter/jumper world I knew so well. Everything here felt so wild and free, as if anything could happen.

Before my nerves got the best of me, we started moving. Russell, the head wrangler, was taking us out for the day. He led us through the creek, past the Old Ainsley Brothers Ranch, and toward the beginning of the Gold Run Trail, where we would stop for lunch and water and let the horses rest before navigating our way up the steep ridge of the trail known as Oh Shit! Ridge.

When we reached the crest of the mountain, Russell stopped the group. He turned to us with a serious expression on his face.

"Okay, gang. There's a reason this part of the ride is called Oh Shit! Ridge."

The guests giggled nervously, and Russell paused. Then he continued.

"It's steep. Above the tree line. Tons of exposure. At the mercy of the elements. And that means things can go wrong—very wrong—quickly. But follow my lead, and we'll get everyone back down the mountain safely."

Russell is one of those true cowboys: loves the horses, loves the land, and is in it for all the right reasons. At the time, I had no idea how intertwined my life would become with Russell, C Lazy U, and everyone who works here. So that day, I simply listened to Russell's direction while enjoying the pure beauty of the surrounding mountains and my sure-footed ranch gelding.

Laura and I, the newbies, weren't intimidated by riding, but we'd never ridden on a trail so steep. So when Russell gently suggested we might prefer to ride toward the middle, I was slightly miffed. But I also reminded myself that my National Horse Show resume didn't automatically qualify me to know how to navigate a narrow ridge in the Colorado Rockies. I consoled myself with the knowledge that even our show horses would have been quaking at the terrain while the confident ranch gelding I sat upon took it all in stride. Swallowing my pride, I followed Russell's suggestion and stayed in the middle of the group.

I glanced over at Laura to gauge how well she was handling this steep and rocky ridge and somewhat pathetic line placement. From the look of her steely glare and the erect riding posture I normally saw her assume only when preparing for a major competition, it was obvious to me that both of our egos were bruised. Realizing I wasn't the only one longing to join the ranks of the more experienced return guests, I made a mental note to scheme with my friend that evening to get Russell to recognize our innate riding talents as quickly as possible so we might be invited to take a more advanced spot in the group later in the week.

As I looked out at the sky, I blinked back tears. *I feel so free out here. A freedom I haven't felt for years. But why the hell does this feel so different? Am I trapped? Is it Reed? Or the firm? Or the law school loans?*

As a child and teen, whenever I asked myself probing, existential questions like this, I just knew what the right answer was—whether it was to stop partying with the guys in high school so I could spend more time in the barn or to refrain from dating the almost thirty-year-old trainer who was making moves on me when I was sixteen and knew full well he'd pay for my hunter/jumper lifestyle if I gave him what he wanted.

But that day, my gut failed me. And that's when I realized how long it had been since I'd checked in with myself in a meaningful way. It had been years since I'd even asked myself deeper questions. I had been so busy being what I thought I needed to be, what made sense, and what was "logical" that I had refused to listen to my heart, my soul, and my inner sense of knowing.

Though I didn't want to admit it, my life had become a grind. But I wasn't alone: it seemed everyone I knew had entered into some imaginary contract upon graduation in which we agreed to enter the Philadelphia rat race in exchange for money, prestige, and power.

Just passed the bar? Don't celebrate for too long because it's time to work your way into a top-tier law firm. And if you get the job at that top-tier firm? Congrats, but get ready to grind out eighty-hour weeks. You gotta prove yourself to the boss if you have any hope of making partner, right? Got yourself a boyfriend? Well, good for you. But is he going to be able to support your lifestyle and give you the 2.5 kids you always wanted, along with the perfectly appointed and remodeled yet still historically accurate Tudor in Radnor or Berwyn?

And here's the kicker: after all that social climbing, working one's ass off, and winning that imaginary trophy called "having it all," it's still quite possible that the blue bloods will still look at that nouveau riche group with disdain.

In that moment, a tiny glimmer of a thought made its way into a forgotten corner of my mind, whispering, *Maybe you're afraid to ask the difficult questions about your life because you're afraid of the answers.*

Sitting on Gunsmoke in the crisp mountain air, I made a pact with myself: *Emme, you're going to do this once a year. Come out here, immerse yourself in the riding, take time to reflect, and figure your shit out.*

We entered a dense aspen forest, and, for a moment, all I could see were tree trunks and greenery. That is, until I noticed a dark mass moving quickly toward the group. As it drew closer, I could make out the silhouette of a moose. And this was no baby.

"Whoaaaaa!" Russell's voice cut through my swirling thoughts and the steady sound of hooves. He maneuvered his horse effortlessly to the left, heading straight for Laura. I turned to see my friend's horse, Caesar, spook suddenly, pivot, and turn erratically like it was doing some convulsive dance. Meanwhile, another horse in the group had responded to Russell's command by stopping dead in its tracks—right in front of Laura and Caesar.

Laura grabbed the reins and pulled with what appeared to be superhuman strength as Caesar skidded to a stop mere inches from the other horse. Laura's impeccable reflexes prevented a full head-on collision that could have seriously injured either horse, either rider, or all four of them. Once Caesar stopped moving, however, inertia threw Laura off the horse. One leg twisted at an unnatural angle as she fell off her steed and hit the ground with a loud thud that was sure to leave more than bruises.

Laura winced and grabbed her leg while Russell continued to make emergency calls to the others so that everyone would move away from the scene of the collision.

Russell jumped off his horse and ran over to Laura. "What the hell, kid?" He growled like a parent who was both angry and scared to death after his child had run out in the middle of the street.

A tear trickled down Laura's cheek. "I dunno what happened, Russell. I, uh, have no idea what got into Caesar . . ."

Russell laughed. "I know *exactly* what happened! You certainly have the equestrian pedigree and ribbons to your name, but that doesn't matter when your horse gets spooked by a moose protecting her baby. Guess you hunter/jumpers aren't used to that scenario."

Laura's saucer eyes remained fixed on the cowboy as he continued.

"I know, I know. You and your friend here made a point to let me know how good you two are at riding. Funny thing is, you two are the best damn riders I've seen all year. Hell, you're both better than some of the staff here. But that's not the point. Out here, we're dealing with the mountain, wild animals, and the elements. We lack control over all those variables, and it's important for you to respect that before I will consider letting any guest—no matter how talented— do anything stupid out here."

Russell drew in a breath and looked up at the sky, as if the wonders of riding at C Lazy U were inextricably linked to the heavens. "There's a strategy, a protocol, and safety measures we take. It looks effortless, but you have no idea how precise I am in leading the group. Just one thing or person," Russell eyed Laura knowingly, "can put the horses and riders in danger in the blink of an eye. Which you just witnessed."

At this point, Laura, who rarely cried, began sobbing and massaging her injured leg. As he took in her reaction, Russell's shoulders relaxed, and his tone softened. "Listen, Laura, you and Emme are 100 percent going to be up front with me by Friday—but you need to trust that there's a reason I put you where I did on day one. Got it?"

Laura bit her lip and nodded.

Russell bent over and gently touched her leg. "Is that where you twisted it?"

"Mm-hmm," Laura replied meekly.

Russell manipulated her leg a bit, and, for a moment, I wondered if he had been a doctor in a previous lifetime. He smiled. "I've seen a million of these during my years as an army medic. Saw it during my time guiding elk hunts in Montana too. It's most likely a slight strain. Nothing that some ice, a cold beer, and maybe even a shot of whiskey won't cure."

Laura looked at Russell incredulously. "Really? That's all you think it is?"

Russell shook his head. "Well, I'm no doctor, but that's my guess. However, I don't take our guests' safety lightly, and we're not taking chances." He grinned. "Kid, we're gonna get you back to the ranch ASAP so a ranch hand can take you to the clinic in town and confirm my hunch that it's a minor strain. If that's the case, I know this type of injury hurts like hell at first. But you'll be amazed what a little ice and Tylenol can do for that. In fact, I'm willing to bet you'll be back in the saddle in no time, and . . ." He paused almost dramatically. "If my instincts are right, you and your friend will be leading the pack by Friday in the way you've been hoping to. But *only* if you follow the doctor's orders, okay?"

Laura smiled and nodded happily, as if Russell had just given her the golden key to a magical city.

Russell turned to me. "Emme, there's no cell service here, so I'm going to ride down the mountain a bit so I can call the general manager and let him know we have an injured rider. He'll send a vehicle and a wrangler out to come get you back down the mountain in one piece. He took a deep breath and turned to my friend. "And Laura?"

She locked eyes with Russell as if bracing for what he was going to say next.

Russell's eyes crinkled at the corners as he let a small grin escape from his lips. "Do me a favor. Have a shot of whiskey ready for me too."

As he walked back toward his horse, he quipped, "Y'know, with you two, I might need more than a shot. In fact, a whole bottle of Jameson might be in order by the end of this week."

CHAPTER 2

STAND AND DELIVER

OCTOBER 14, 2020
5:00 PM

The tack room buzzed with nervous tension. Kyra, Allison, Kai, Jessica, Lexi, Molly, and the rest of the wranglers were whispering among themselves but stopped as I entered the room, falling completely silent—like a record stopping at a junior high dance. All eyes bore into me. Some of the girls looked curious, but most looked annoyed. Five o'clock staff meetings were not their thing—especially when they were ready to pack up and go home for the night.

Tom stood behind me, as if to communicate that he was standing by my side and believed in me, but that this was my rodeo.

It's good Tom has faith in me right now, because I sure don't! I've been head wrangler without Russell for less than three years, and now I may need to make the decision of the century.

I drew in a deep breath and exhaled slowly, reminding myself that if I wavered, I'd lose the group. *Just like with horses, they sense nervousness and hesitation. But as long as you have their best interests at heart, those horses will follow—and they will forgive you, even if you don't ride perfectly that day. These girls are the same: committed and in need of someone to unify them. If you have their best interests at heart, they'll follow—and they will forgive you too, even if you don't make the perfect decisions or deliver the news in the perfect way.*

"Girls, I've got some bad news. Even though the fire is still well over fifteen miles away, the smoke has made its way here. I know it's not too bad here—yet—but things *could* get worse. And if the smoke continues to get heavier, we may need to cancel rides tomorrow. So, to remain transparent, Jack wants me to speak with the guests and suggest some alternate activities, just in case."

Allison's look of shock mirrored the sentiment of the group. "Emme, some of the guests get annoyed when they can't ride *more*. And while I 100 percent agree that we can't put the horses in danger, it's not just *you* who will be dealing with their anger if you share this tidbit of information. It's not like we've canceled anything yet, so why alarm anyone? We're all going to take the heat for this *announcement*," she said, making air quotes, "you plan to make."

The other girls nodded, clearly in agreement with Allison as she continued. "And I, for one, have taken enough heat from Justin lately. Now you're telling me I need to deal with the Radshaws over the slight chance that a ride or two might be canceled?"

The Radshaws were one of the ranch's most profitable— and most demanding—clients. Not only did their four kids keep Nicole's hands full all day long, but Glen and Belinda Radshaw were blissfully ignorant about anything grounded in reality. In their posh world, everyone else existed on the edges to serve their latest whims. Caviar at midnight? If Belinda craved it, there was absolutely no reason the staff shouldn't drive through the night to find some. And if Glen decided he didn't want to follow the no-smoking rule in the lodge dining room? The other guests should sit outside if they didn't like it. I mean, Glen smoked only the *best* cigars, and who wouldn't appreciate that?

But even with their somewhat entitled idiosyncrasies, I loved the Radshaws—along with all the other families that came back to the C Lazy U year after year. By this point in my career, they were almost like an extended family of my own.

And families take care of one another. So I should give them a heads-up. Shouldn't I?

I knew Allison had a point. The guests might overreact, and maybe I was being paranoid about something that wasn't even sure to happen. But I also sensed that Revenge Allison might be poised to strike. That was my name for the person she morphed into when her love life hit a bump in the road. Clearly, the shelf life of her relationship with Justin had expired, and now the rest of us were going to take the brunt of her anger and vengeance. Instead of sneaking away from the group to cry like Kyra did or drowning her sorrows in whiskey and beer like Lexi would, Allison worked through her feelings by lambasting anyone in her path. Anyone, that is, except the person she should have aimed her anger at: Justin.

But it wasn't just Revenge Allison that worried me; even when she was happy with her love life, Allison's life growing up on a cattle ranch in Wyoming had made her into a rough-around-the-edges woman. Even on her best days, she was a true Western cowgirl, prepared to fight at a moment's notice. Clearly, my news was triggering that fighting spirit—and if I wasn't careful, she would soon have the rest of the girls in her camp.

I nodded and did my best to empathize with her and the other girls. "I get it. But, ladies, we can't put the horses in danger, and I owe it to the guests to give them a heads-up. So let's compromise. If the Radshaws start up with you or anyone else," I turned to the other girls, "just hand them off to me. I'll take care of them so the rest of you can deal with the more sane guests. Deal?"

Allison opened her mouth, clearly poised to rebut my offer. But she must've thought better of it. She nodded, and the rest of the girls followed suit.

"Okay, then. I guess it's time to tell them." I started toward the door and then shared the other bit of information I was dreading. "One other thing. If the conditions really do get worse—as in more than just the smoke—we may be doing more than canceling rides . . ."

My voice drifted off. I couldn't yet bring myself to say we'd have to evacuate the guests and possibly even the horses.

Fortunately, no further words were necessary. My girls were street-smart enough to know what I implied. Yet I also knew they thought I was being Henny-Penny-the-sky-is-falling, overreactive Emme. By playing up my paranoia and tendency to panic, they could rationalize their own fears by living in an optimistic fantasyland and pretending that this fire, which was apparently worsening by the minute, would magically disappear and we could all return to normalcy.

Everyone filed out of the room, and Tom made the announcement over the radio that all staff should direct the guests to the lodge dining room for a meeting about the fire.

5:30 PM

I picked up a spoon and a glass of water from the nearest table, then clinked the two together as if I were going to make a wedding toast.

I cleared my throat, trying to think of the best way to start.

Screw it, Emme, just speak from the heart.

"Hi, everyone. It's good to see everybody in the same room together."

I paused, a trick I'd learned in the courtroom to build anticipation and capture the jury's interest and attention.

"Since Jack is at a meeting in town with the Granby fire chief, he asked me to speak with everyone. As you know, the wildfire is still some distance away, but we owe it to you, the horses, and the safety of our staff to consider contingency plans in the event conditions worsen here. With that being said, and in the interest of transparency, our general manager wanted me to let you know that if the smoke makes its way to the ranch, we may need to cancel the morning rides. When there's too much smoke in the air, it just isn't safe for anyone, horses and guests included. Of course, this all depends on the track of the fire. And while conditions could worsen over the next twenty-four hours, nobody knows for sure . . ."

My voice trailed off, this time more to gauge the tenor of the room than to build anticipation. The deafening silence told me everything I needed to know: speaking from the heart was not what this group needed. And whipping the crowd into a nervous frenzy was the last thing Jack gave me permission to do.

The wranglers want to operate under the assumption that this is all going to go away, and our guests may be feeling the same. Maybe the girls were right: I'm worrying everyone needlessly. And while Jack did give me permission to speak to them this evening, it was only with the understanding that we were being overly cautious in the announcement. He made it abundantly clear that any official warnings, evacuations, canceled rides, or major decisions would come from him. Time to dial it back. I'm coming across way too intensely.

This was no time to throw everyone into a panic, no matter how nervous I was. Besides, if I could keep things light and easy, that would give us more time behind the scenes to plan.

I assumed another fake smile and brightened my tone as much as I could. "So, I want to start by thanking you for being *such* amazing guests and good sports about this! To be honest, this meeting is just a reminder that C Lazy U *always* delivers good times and memories, no matter what!"

I turned to the staff, who had no idea where I was going with this. *Hell, I don't know what I'm talking about!* But everyone played along and nodded in agreement.

I paused again to gauge how my message was landing with the guests. Some still appeared somber, but the rest seemed to visibly relax. Some even seemed slightly annoyed with this inconvenient predinner meeting, while others were obviously nonplussed. A few began scrolling on their phones, as if this was not that big of a deal.

Good. They're relaxed. Jack would kill me if I freaked everyone out.

I continued. "We aim to please. And you know we always have so many events and activities planned, in addition to riding. So, in the *very* slim chance that we would need to adjust any of the riding plans or outdoor activities at any point tomorrow or later in the week, Jack wanted me to let you all know that he is adding more indoor activities to the schedule for your pleasure."

That got their attention. "In addition to his regularly scheduled class, Chef Antonio and his culinary team will be offering mini cooking classes to groups of eight during the day, on the hour, every hour, starting at ten a.m. Meanwhile, our sommelier, Steven (*Yes, I work at a dude ranch with a sommelier*), will be conducting wine tasting every thirty minutes. The top of the hour will focus on whites, and on the half hour, you can learn more about our amazing selection of reds! And at six p.m., a special champagne edition. Once again, this all begins tomorrow."

I had no idea where these ideas were coming from—or if our staff could even do what I was promising!—but somehow, staying calm and positive seemed more than necessary. It felt critical. I crossed my fingers behind my back, hoping Jack would be okay with my impromptu ideas.

Can't forget about the kids! "Now, for the kiddos. Nicole is going to continue with the art projects, but she's agreed to a twist: edible crafts! I'll keep the details a secret." I winked at the parents, and a few of the children who had tagged along let out squeals of delight.

Nicole, Antonio, and Steven sat up straight at the mention of their names and thankfully rose to my impromptu challenge in the moment.

Antonio piped up. "I know this is new and different, but I think the regulars will enjoy learning some secret ranch recipes!"

I glanced over at the three of them, certain they were madly trying to think of what they were going to do to deliver on my promises. The creativity of this team was always impressive.

I turned to Lucas, who was covering for Tom in his absence. Now he sat up straight, as if preparing himself for what I might say about his crew.

"Finally, for those of you who don't ride but enjoy outdoor sports, the activity guides will coordinate shuttles over to the Fraser Rec Center for some indoor rock climbing as another option. You can burn a sweat without having to breathe in some of the smoke that's out there. Sign-ups will begin at the front desk shortly for you to make your alternate selections. If you have any questions, let me know. Have a wonderful dinner and enjoy your evening, everyone!"

As the guests trickled out of the room, I could hear them discussing their options. A few people lingered behind to chat with one another. Nicole asked Antonio if he had gummy worms, pudding, and graham crackers. "We can make worms-in-dirt cups. Kids love that!" she said. Meanwhile, Steven was already behind the bar, arranging wineglasses and bottles.

Smiling inwardly, I knew this was the right way to handle it. Even though I was already tired from trying to fake enthusiasm for the activities, I knew if I could distract everyone sufficiently, I could refocus on the fire—and start reviewing Russell's evacuation plan.

5:45 PM

She had been lingering in a corner, but as soon as the majority of the guests cleared the room, I watched in horror as Belinda Radshaw entered the room and made a beeline toward Allison and me, a look of righteous indignation on her fresh-from-the-spa exfoliated face. Her voice carried across the high-ceilinged room as she approached.

"Do you have any idea how difficult this will be on Benjamin, Bella, Brady, and Glen Junior? They can't wait for the rides each day. And because of some stupid wildfire, you're telling me they might need to stay inside and do lame arts and crafts? We came to the ranch to ride, not do crafts!"

Allison raised her shoulders and clenched her fists. *Easy, Allison,* I silently prayed as Belinda got closer.

Anyone who spent five minutes with Allison knew that

one of her biggest pet peeves was entitlement—making it ironic that she worked here, the epitome of privilege and wealth. However, her choice stemmed from the desire to advance her horse career by starting her own dude ranch with her family—a dream that her parents felt could be realized only after she spent some time at C Lazy U to learn more. I knew that if Allison could have it her way, she would work exclusively with the cattle and horses, not people. But I also knew customer service was the part she needed to work on the most, so I did my best to keep her involved with the guests—even if it meant having to constantly monitor her reactions when a guest triggered her.

Take a breath, Allison! You can do it.

But Allison's impulse control was not much better than a preschooler's. She muttered under her breath, "You think *I* created the wildfire? Suck it up. Your worst day is better than most people's best ones. Find a real problem in your first world—"

Belinda, potentially within earshot at this point, raised her perfectly shaped eyebrows and said, "Are you talking to me? What did you just say?"

"Mrs. Radshaw," I interrupted. Taking a gamble that Belinda had been too far away to hear Allison clearly, I lied. "Sorry about that. Allison was talking to *me*."

Belinda crossed her arms and locked eyes with me. I couldn't be sure, but my gut told me she was merely irritated and hadn't heard what Allison said. So I continued.

"I know how excited your kids are about riding. And like I said, I'm 99 percent sure the show will go on as usual." I smiled nervously, hoping Belinda would accept my customer-service-style apology.

Belinda sniffed. "I know it's not your fault, but the *children* get so excited. And now, to think I might be dealing with whining during the rest of the trip? *Puh-leese.*" She drew out the words *children* and *please* dramatically, as if this potential change in plans would put her offspring (and her) in complete peril.

Allison opened her mouth, and I put my hand on her shoulder to remind her I was still standing right there. Then I said, "I understand, and I am truly sorry for this. Obviously, it's beyond our control. But I promise you that if worst comes to worst, we will be 100 percent committed to getting your kids back in the saddle as soon as we can! The smoke may be just too thick for the horses to exert themselves. And Nicole would do her absolute best to take the kids' minds off any canceled rides."

I turned to Allison. "Allison, if you could tend to the Detwilers, I would appreciate it. Please make sure they know where to sign up for the additional activities." The Detwiler family had been coming to the ranch for over a decade, but they were the opposite of the Radshaws: unassuming, effusive with compliments, and never demanding. And they tipped really well.

Always ready with a comeback, Allison opened her mouth,

I'm sure to argue that the Detwilers didn't need assistance—which was true. But when she saw the expression on my face, she seemed to think better of it and said, "Fine, Emme."

Across the room, Glen Radshaw was furiously pointing to the glass of wine on the bar. Belinda giggled. "He knows I hate warm Chardonnay." She turned back to me. "I know you'll do your best to make it work. Thanks, Emme." Then she waved as she walked toward her husband and called, "Coming, honey!"

With Belinda gone, I put my hand on Allison's shoulder. As she turned to face me, I started talking, not giving her a chance to say anything.

"I told you, *I* take care of the Radshaws. The only thing you say to them from here on out is, 'Emme, can I assist you with that?' Got it?"

Allison glared. "Emme, it's not my fault you're an overreactive East Coast lawyer who thinks *this* wildfire is somehow different from the others. You're not used to living through the fires, but I was born and bred in Wyoming, and wildfires have been a part of my entire life. In case you haven't noticed, I'm not alone in my opinion either."

My stomach tightened with the realization that she was right. They had no idea that even Jack was taking this seriously because he wanted to be the one to break the news. So there I was, looking like an overly anxious East Coast transplant, trying to tell the ranch OGs what this fire was going to do next.

But defending myself wasn't going to work; it never

worked with Allison. She was too much of a fighter, so she would meet anything that appeared defensive with more verbal sparring. I pivoted and focused on her Revenge Allison side, which was rearing its ugly head, even though I knew it was coming from a place of sorrow.

"I know you think I'm being crazy," I said. "And you may be right. I also know you're in a rough spot, and I'm sorry about Justin." That's when the anger on Allison's face dissipated as tears glistened in her eyes. I had touched a nerve—and the root of her outburst. "Listen," I continued. "We've got a potentially serious situation on our hands, so I need to ask you to dig deep and put your feelings aside for a few days so we can get through this—together."

The words *together* and *Allison* did not go hand in hand, considering that she had always had an attitude with me. In fact, when Russell retired, Allison was shocked that he recommended me before the other, much more experienced wranglers. From that moment forward, I could tell that whenever Allison asked me a question, her intention was less about seeking an answer and more about trying to make me look wrong or misinformed.

I'm sure that's why Russell had given me his sage advice before his departure: "Treat her—and all the other wranglers—in the same way you treat the horses, Emme. Don't push too hard. If you push—you know, if she starts to get tense or come at you—you need to back up, relax, and approach her in a softer way."

Russell was right. The less pressure I applied, the more she would respond, just like Trigger or Dually or Josie. Maybe a bit grudgingly at first, but eventually, she'd come around and do what was best for the team.

She was in the wrong, but I didn't need to belabor that point. By pulling back, I communicated to Allison that I understood she was hurting. I didn't need to add more pressure than I already had.

Allison bit her lower lip and gave me a sad smile. "I hate to say this, but you're right. That little outburst of mine was more about Justin than Belinda Radshaw. I'm sorry. I need to work on that." She paused. "I hate to admit it, but now I know why my dad sent me out here. If I pulled that shit with someone on their ranch, he'd lay me out to pasture."

Wow. I had never once heard Allison apologize—no matter how wrong she was. *And self-reflection? Insight? Taking responsibility for her actions? Guess there's a first time for everything.* I silently thanked Russell for his nugget of wisdom.

"But, Emme. This doesn't change the fact that you're totally overreacting. We *are* going to be riding tomorrow. Mark my words."

And just like that, the moment of bonding was gone. Before I could even respond to Allison's dig, my phone started vibrating. This time, it was a text from Jack:

Call me when you're finished talking to the guests. It's urgent.

BCLU

SPRING 2007

"A dude ranch? Laura, you can't be serious! What happened to our warm, tropical getaways?"

But she was totally serious. Laura, my best friend (and most down-to-earth friend from my junior hunter days), nodded. "Emme, this is no ordinary dude ranch. I went there for years when I was a kid, and it's indescribable. But as an adult? Even more amazing! It's a whole experience: spa, five-star gourmet dining, hiking, firepits, and wine tastings. It's like glamping with horses!"

As I took in that information, she quipped, "Not only that, but we can actually ride—and you can't say that about every-one who goes there. The riding is absolutely incredible. We'll be able to gallop through fields and ride to our hearts' con-tent. Those cowgirls and cowboys won't know how to handle us English girls!" Laura crossed her arms and grinned, point-ing at all the ribbons hanging on the wall of my home office.

I laughed, figuring she was probably right. What would a cowboy know about the world of A-rated hunter/jumper shows, custom Vogel boots, Tailored Sportsman breeches, and perfectly tailored riding jackets? Then again, I would need to go out and buy some Wranglers, cowboy hats, and boots—something totally foreign to me.

Laura lowered her voice to a whisper. "Plus, it might be good for you to get away from Reed for a week."

Ah, yes. Reed. I peered across the hall and took in the sight of my passed-out fiancé, whose penchant for wine and video games ("My art," Reed argued) consumed most of his waking hours. He spent the rest of his hours exactly as he was now: passed out on the designer couch that two twentysomethings could afford only with his family's seemingly endless stream of gifts and money.

Of course, Reed couldn't help that he was born into a privileged family. He couldn't help that his dad became the CEO of one of the fastest-growing hedge fund companies—originally a one-office operation in Philadelphia but had offices popping up all over the globe and corporate headquarters in Manhattan. He couldn't help that his dad was able to pay me a six-figure salary to offer the firm legal opinions as long as I didn't mind shuttling between Philadelphia and New York. And he couldn't help that his doting mother encouraged every whim of his with plenty of time and money to pursue whatever struck his fancy that day, week, or month.

If I'm being completely honest with myself, this was the allure of Reed. Sure, my engineer dad and nurse mother made decent salaries as the parents of an only child in the Philadelphia suburbs, but nothing can compare with the kind of bank Reed's family made. I was pretty sure his dad could put even my wealthiest old-money friends to shame—or at least compete with them. And I'm pretty sure if Reed had ever expressed an interest in horses—he didn't, but oh, how I wish he had!—his family would've gifted him (or me) the fanciest horse of his choice, the best trainers, and all the time and money in the world to travel, show, and jump.

That was Reed's world and his reality: Reed wanted something, Reed got it. Immediately.

And it wasn't enough that Reed got everything he wanted. He had to take it one step further by controlling what he didn't want others to have—including anything I liked. That's why he made it a point to convince his parents that horses were an absurd habit. "Such a waste of time and money!" he would lament, as if his parents might spend less on him if they thought they should invest in that "dumb sport." I've got to hand it to him: his power of persuasion prevailed, considering nobody in his family so much as mentioned anything equine-related in conversation, *ever*.

Laura handed me the glossy brochure, and I turned the trifold over, glancing at the weekly rates.

"Don't worry," she reassured me. "This is my dad's treat."

"Oh, no, Laura," I protested. "I'm a lawyer making a perfectly decent salary—not a charity case!"

Never one to lose an argument—a throwback to her debate team days—Laura laughed. "He insists. In fact, he said if you go, it's more like a gift to *him*. He knows how much I loved these trips—not to mention that he knows how much stress I've been under, trying to navigate this lease agreement while running a company."

On the heels of a nasty breakup, Laura had moved back into her parents' McMansion in Wayne as a very temporary measure. As the vice president of a money management firm, she could have lived wherever she wanted. But my common-sense friend had no patience or time to find a place while she waited on the unit she had her eye on while in the midst of her busiest time of year. The ultramodern Rittenhouse One checked all her boxes when it came to accoutrements and amenities, but the old lady whose lease was up the next month couldn't decide if her teacup Maltese would be able to make the transition to the newer, even more luxe Rittenhouse Two.

Laura repeated for what I think was the millionth time, "I swear, if I can't move into Rittenhouse One because some octogenarian's six-pound dog will get 'too anxious' about having to shit and piss in a new location that's *literally one block away*, I really need to question my life choices!"

I laughed a bit too loudly, rousing Reed from his wine-induced slumber.

"Hey, babe," he slurred as he rose to his feet and made his way to the door of the office. Noticing Laura, he snarled. The two of them had never gotten along, and neither one made a secret of that.

"Hi, Reed." Laura's icy tone chilled the room.

"Oh. Hi, Laura," Reed muttered. "Sorry to hear about Lance. He was a great guy."

I felt my face flush as I thought, *Great guy? You hated Lance. You had nothing good to say about Lance except he had good taste in cigars. You're just saying this to Laura to be an ass.*

Laura winced. The hurt was too fresh and raw—but Reed didn't notice. Or didn't care. Or both.

"I mean it, Laura. What'd ya do to make this one run? OCD? Poor guy couldn't pass the white-glove test? Or, no. Lemme guess. It's that crazy work schedule. I mean, how many eighty-hour weeks do you really need to work?"

He laughed at what he perceived to be witty while Laura's jaw clenched in anger and disgust.

As someone who despises conflict, I typically tried to smooth things over between the two of them. Make peace. Remain the calming force. But Reed had gone too far, and Laura was in no emotional state to fend for herself.

"Back off, Reed," I warned.

He laughed. "Or what? What are you gonna do about it?"

I took a deep breath and exhaled slowly, measuring my words before speaking. *He's not in his right mind right now, and arguing gets us nowhere.* "You're in no place to judge, so just let Laura and me talk. Okay?"

Realizing he wasn't going to get a rise out of either one of us, Reed rolled his eyes and retreated to the living room sofa, mumbling something about cabernet and *Halo* graphics. Within seconds, his rumbling snores filled the apartment.

Laura turned to me. "Thanks, Em. For being a lawyer, you are the least argumentative person on the planet outside the courtroom. So for you to tell Reed to lay off, you must be *pissed.*" She lowered her voice again and said, "And you have every reason to be! You deserve better, Emme, and you know it."

Tears filled my eyes as the truth of Laura's words worked their way into my heart.

Not one to cry herself and being uncomfortable around anyone who might, Laura politely excused herself, explaining that she had an early day at work and needed some sleep. "Think about the ranch, Emme. It would be so much fun!"

I smiled at my dear friend and nodded. "Okay, I'll let you know soon. 'Night, Laura."

No sooner than I'd closed the door, my phone chirped. It was a text from Reed's dad. Even though he'd hired me, a text from him was unusual. I had little to no contact with him at work, as I spent most of my days working with the VPs and other lawyers.

Dear Emme,
Please check your email when you get a chance. I think it
will make you smile.
Sincerely,
Alfred

It always made me giggle to see the older generation texting as if they were handwriting a letter to put in some sort of digital mail. Curious, I logged into the company server and clicked on my inbox. As I read Alfred's message, the full import of what everyone at work had been gossiping about hit me: they'd landed the huge account from Germany, and they needed me in an even more active role now. That meant more lawyers would join the team—and they wanted *me* to join the newly formed legal department as one of the lead attorneys. Alfred even added the potential salary range that the board would be willing to entertain, and the numbers were what I had only dreamed about during all those sleepless nights I'd spent studying for the bar. And now, Emme Lee Muller—novice lawyer—was essentially being handed an offer too good to refuse on a silver platter!

I paused, waiting for that thrilling feeling of elation to wash over me.

Nothing.

Why don't I feel happy?

I willed my brain to weigh the pros and cons of the situation.

Pros: More money, more responsibility, more prestige, better legal connections that could lead to even bigger prospects in the future, the chance to hone my leadership skills, and having a voice in the direction the firm takes in making monumental decisions at a pivotal time, with extremely important clients. And when it comes to my horse habit, more money to ride— and maybe even be able to afford showing in the amateur owner division again and maybe even the jumpers.

Cons? Not practicing the type of law I wanted to practice, less time to ride, there would be no time for anything but work—and making the commitment to remain with a company in Reed's family, which all but seals my fate with him. Of course, we're getting married, but there can be no pre-wedding jitters or second thoughts if his father is giving me the opportunity of a lifetime!

Usually, my pro/con list would make my decision an easy one, but what appeared to be a win-win kept feeling like a lose-lose, no matter which choice I made. I felt even more like I was drowning in someone else's life when all I really wanted was the freedom I found while riding.

Crushing career with great money and no time to enjoy it. Isn't there more to life than that?

But . . .

If I left it all, I would have time to ride.

But . . .

Would it be worth the sacrifice to give up everything I worked so hard for?

But . . .

I'd be broke. How would I afford horses then, especially with those ridiculously high student loan payments? Where else am I going to make this kind of money?

In a moment of uncharacteristic impulsiveness, I decided *not* to decide that night. Instead, I'd make a different choice: stop worrying about everyone else for today and make one small decision that would make *me* happy.

Trade in the pencil skirts and high heels for a week of cowboy hats, boots, and fancy ranch quarter horses? Right about now, that sounds heavenly.

After texting Alfred a profuse *Thank you so much! Let's discuss tomorrow!* I clicked on my text thread with Laura and typed:

Okay, you win. You need a break from work—and that lady with the small dog. And I need a break from work and Reed. Let me know when to put in my vacation days, and let's go!

CHAPTER 3

AN AFFAIR TO FORGET

OCTOBER 15, 2020

8:00 AM

I was struggling to breathe, and the waves of nausea were getting worse. Usually, my drive through the arched entrance of C Lazy U filled me with a feeling of homecoming. But today, I felt only dread. I looked to the sky and silently cursed the menacing, looming clouds of smoke.

Opening the car door only made things worse. I slammed it shut. *How can the horses breathe? This is significantly worse than yesterday.*

I squinted through stinging, watery eyes as I retrieved my phone from my purse. I immediately called Jack and started rambling at the sound of his voice.

"We can't ride today! It's only gotten worse. Like, how did the horses even make it through the night? I've been here less than thirty seconds, and my eyes are burning. My lungs feel like I smoked a pack of cigarettes with the car windows rolled up! You thought things were urgent last night? This is on a whole new level . . ."

I stopped to catch my breath and watched a family walk toward the lodge, holding their T-shirts up to their faces like makeshift masks. "This is not good for the guests either," I added.

Before he could respond, I wavered, playing devil's advocate with myself and thinking out loud. Maybe I was being emotional. Maybe I was still exaggerating.

"Then again," I said, "the Williams Fork Fire and Cameron Peak Fire burned all summer. I know this one is closer, but maybe the fire chief has just been putting a scare into us so we don't blow it off. You know what we say: the show must go on."

Jack cleared his throat, and I could tell he was measuring his words carefully. "Emme. Things could get bad. Really bad. In fact, so bad that the owners are prepared to deal with the ramifications of closing the ranch altogether and sending the guests home."

Send them home? I tried to put myself in Jack's shoes. *He's talking about thousands and thousands of vacation dollars. Hell, keeping a full staff on payroll could be a challenge, depending on how long we need to close down. And not to mention, we need the money to feed the horses. But if we don't send people packing, it sounds like we're risking a whole lot more than money. We're playing with people's lives.*

Jack continued. "Listen, you already called Dr. Hecksher, and she agreed if the smoke got worse—which it has—that you're not being overly dramatic. The effect this smoke could have on the horses *is* significant. And to be honest, if we can't ride, we're cheating the guests out of the main reason 99 percent of them come here. It's not fair to them."

Wow. The realization that Jack was willing to risk losing so much money hit me—hard. *This fire might be as bad as we feared!* I opened my mouth to speak, only to be interrupted again.

"Hang on, Emme. It's the Granby fire chief."

As soon as Jack put me on hold, I crossed my fingers and even said a little prayer. "Okay, God. I know I don't talk to you often, but *please* give Jack some good news! Maybe it's not as bad as we thought. Or maybe we cancel this week, and then, when the smoke clears, we can reopen next week."

I heard the click of Jack's line switching back over. "As if things can't get any worse, the Granby fire chief just told me that while we are not under an official pre-evacuation order, I'd be negligent if we *didn't* evacuate the guests, pronto. It's not much of a choice at this point."

This was one time I so badly wanted to be wrong. There was absolutely no satisfaction in this horrible confirmation of my gut instincts—that the fire was going to get worse, not better.

"When does the chief suggest we evacuate the guests?" I asked.

"Now."

"Like, right now? Jack, you've got to give me a few hours, at least!"

"I'm going to meet with the guests. Explain why everyone needs to leave and then handle all the financial questions, as well as work with the front desk to help people switch their flights and coordinate shuttles to Denver International. In the meantime, I need you to start implementing our fire plan for the animals."

The fire plan Jack was referring to was *not* an option. The old ranch plan I found crumpled on a piece of yellow paper in the back of one of Russell's filing cabinets was to cut the fence, open the irrigation ditches, flood the meadows, and push the horses to the reservoir. If necessary, we could jingle them over Curtis Ridge—a high ridge on the northeast side—to get them out of harm's way.

Just cutting a fence and letting the horses run free sounded like outdated cowboy crap. It wasn't an airtight plan in the least. Those horses were like my children, and this plan would be a death wish for our most vulnerable animals.

I couldn't allow that to happen. Not on my watch.

"With all due respect, that fire plan doesn't consider the donkeys," I said. "Or sick horses. Or the oldest ones. Or our new two-week-old foal and his mom. There's no way they would survive if we just started cutting fences. But if you can give me an hour or two, I know we can get the highest-priority animals out first. And then we will worry about the rest of the herd once we get the official pre-evacuation order—without having to cut the fence."

Although I had been internally strategizing for the past twenty-four hours, there was a part of me that couldn't bring myself to believe that moment might arrive—when we would really be called to evacuate more than two hundred horses.

How on earth are we going to move them? And where?

9:30 AM

Before Tom could explain anything more to me about the fire, Kyra approached the two of us. Her eyebrows were raised in fear, emphasizing her flawless eyelash extensions and piercing emerald eyes. A Florida native who'd shown in the pony hunters before becoming a barrel racer, Kyra had matured into an amazing wrangler who somehow blended her love of Southern prep fashion with the rugged demands of ranch life. She had been working for me for just about two years.

"Emme, what's the problem?" she asked, bluntly inter-rupting. She nervously tugged at her chaps, probably trying to make sure they emphasized all the right curves.

I glanced over Kyra's shoulder to see Joey, a seasonal fly-fishing guide who had taken up bronc riding that past summer at the local rodeo, taking stock of her perfectly proportioned frame. Since we'd been short-staffed the past few weeks, Joey agreed to join our team temporarily. Not only did we need the extra assistance in the barn, but he was a damn good rider to boot. If the situation hadn't been so dire, I might have even laughed at the preposterousness of the situation: there we were, dealing with what might be a historic wildfire, and all these two cared about was how someone's ass looked in chaps and denim.

It was no secret that Kyra was hooking up with Joey. We saw their sideways glances and heard the inside jokes. Plus, there were too many occasions to count when everyone was sidled up at Charlie's Bar during Saturday night karaoke, asking, "Where are Kyra and Joey?" only to see them saunter in twenty minutes later, red-faced and smiling.

But Kyra wasn't the only one enamored with Joey. Between his charisma and charm, it was easy to understand why the summer photographer had plastered his contagious smile all over C Lazy U PR materials and social media pages—and why any pretty lady was more than happy to give him the time of day (and sometimes more than that). Kyra must've known about this side of Joey, but what was still unknown was if she thought his wandering eyes—and possibly other wandering parts—were over.

But that was not any of my business, just like none of Kyra's other sexual escapades were any of my business— despite the fact that she couldn't seem to help herself in sharing the most intimate details of every encounter she had with her cowboy of the week (or month).

Except for Joey. None of the girls would judge her for hooking up with him. But for some reason, Kyra remained eerily quiet about him. Even when guests (a.k.a., middle-aged cougars) gushed about "that new cowboy," Kyra went radio silent. The mention of Joey's name transformed her gift of gab into a stony silence that she filled with frenetic activity, whether it was suddenly tending to a horse, anxiously retying the ribbons in her long braids, or adjusting the buckle on her chaps, which didn't need any adjusting in the first place.

"The fire," I began. "The fire chief told Jack that the fire continues to gain momentum and grew another few thousand acres last night. There is a strong possibility that the ranch may go under a pre-evacuation order. It might be time to evacuate some of the animals."

Kyra's glossy lips formed an O as she wound a lock of blond hair around her index finger. "Like, evacuate right now?"

"Well, yes, some of them." Instantly, I regretted my decision to answer her honestly. Not only was Kyra one of the most anxious girls I've ever known, but her hypochondriac tendencies caused her to think she was constantly on the verge of death. From a mole she was sure was melanoma to the pulled muscle she was certain was the first sign of a heart attack, Kyra's fear of death was off-the-charts crazy—until she sat on a horse. In those moments, her entire persona would shift into this graceful, fierce woman who rode a horse as if she'd been born on horseback. She was naturally gifted, and her riding was a beautiful dance, graceful and with a quiet confidence that rendered me speechless. The horses always reacted beautifully to the way she rode.

Stupid, Emme. You just told Kyra something that could put her life in mortal danger. It doesn't matter if the fire is still miles away. It doesn't matter if it's just a worst-case scenario at the moment. She's going to freak out and terrify everyone.

I put my arm around Kyra's lean yet muscular shoulder—noticing how hard her arms had become from tacking up hundreds of ranch horses all summer long—and lowered my voice, trying to sound as reassuring and confident as possible.

"Look. We need to stay calm, okay? Everything is going to be all right—we just need to be prepared and start moving everyone to safety. But if we panic, we won't be able to think clearly, and *that* would be dangerous. Got it?"

Kyra extended her right arm around me and squeezed my waist, as if she would remain safe as long as she held on tight to someone.

"Okay," she said, taking a few deep breaths to calm her overwhelming anxiety. "You're right. We need to do everything we can to stay safe. So, what do we do?"

To that question, I had no immediate answer. But I needed to say something. "Kyra, I need you to go tell one of the guys—like Joey—what's happening. But tell him to keep it on the DL, okay?"

There. Getting Kyra to refocus on Joey might help distract her from the actual problem.

She allowed a half smile to escape and whispered, "You got it, Emme! What should I tell him?"

"Tell Joey to coordinate with Allison and Lexi. They need to start preparing the older, sick, and injured horses for evacuation. Also, the three donkeys. They're already starting to show signs of stress from the fire. Have Joey hook up our truck and trailer and get ready to start moving horses to Dr. Hecksher's ranch. She's in the next town over. Thanks, Kyra!"

With that, I watched her tall frame move across the room as she approached Joey, cupped her hand, and whispered in his ear. Joey's face went from his smug I've-still-got-the-charm expression to a momentary look of panic. He turned toward Kyra and looked deep into her eyes as he whispered something back. I couldn't be sure, but it looked like he mouthed, "I love you." No matter. Still none of my business—except that whatever he said did the trick. Kyra's posture relaxed, and she gave me a thumbs-up.

With that dramatic disaster averted, I was fairly confident she wasn't going to tell the rest of the staff we were all in danger of being engulfed in flames. So I turned to Tom.

"Can you imagine how she would have reacted if I told her that Jack is going to tell the guests they need to leave the ranch by noon?"

11:00 AM

Joey and I gave Petey, Tilly, and Wilbur kisses on their noses before unloading them from the trailer at Dr. Hecksher's ranch. I could tell Joey was exhausted, considering this was his fourth trip to our trustworthy vet. I reached out and hugged Dr. Hecksher for the third time that morning.

"Thank you *so* much for letting us use your pens for the donkeys!" I said.

Dr. Hecksher gave me that reassuring smile that all doctors must learn in veterinary school to relax nervous pet parents. "Of course! It's my pleasure to take this worry off your plate. Go, dear, and take care of the horses. The four of us will be fine!"

I knew Dr. Hecksher was right. Our lovable yet mischievous donkeys had a tendency to escape from all the pastures by skirting under the fence. Under Dr. Hecksher's watch and with her pens, there was no danger of that happening.

The wind had already shifted, and the smoke was

lessening. Now satisfied that the donkeys were safe, I felt a sense of relief that everything was under control. Driving back to the ranch, I considered how we would move the rest of the herd. We had already successfully moved Dixi and Shoshone, two old kids' ponies both riddled with arthritis, to Dr. Hecksher's, along with Katie, our old lead line pony, new mom Joy, and two-week-old Remi. Bae and Evinrude weren't old, but Bae had just had a procedure to address a tendon injury, while Evinrude had a bad knee and an acute eye infection that needed twenty-four-hour care. All were safe and sound at Dr. Hecksher's. *But what about the rest?*

When I returned to the ranch, I approached Molly, who was busy tending to a puncture wound on one of the Percheron crosses. As usual, Molly was going way beyond the call of duty. When I first learned she was a wealthy hunter/jumper rider from Cali, I could barely believe it; her demure, humble nature was not something I was used to from that world. But Molly was different. On a personal quest to learn everything she could to become the best horsewoman ever, she figured what better place to learn than on a dude ranch, where she could interact with two hundred horses on any given day. Originally a colt starter for me, Molly had recently extended her contract for another six months, something that made me feel like I hit the lottery on a daily basis! She had truly become my right-hand cowgirl.

"Thanks for all your help, Molly. I really appreciate it. But you really need to get some rest."

She stroked the horse's mane and smiled. "Are you sure? I can help if you need something. Plus, I'm already here."

I patted Molly on the back. "Well, you need to eat or rest—or both! I can't have you wasting away!"

Molly's eyes grew wide. "Oh, no! Is the fire getting worse?"

"Actually, no. If anything, the conditions seem to be improving. So let's take a breather. But God forbid, if anything changes, we'll be rested. And ready."

9:00 PM

"My phone is blowing up!"

Tom poked his head out of the bathroom, the steam from his shower wafting above his head, and asked, "What's up, babe?"

I shook my head in disbelief. "All these people offering to help move the horses if we need help. Amazing."

The relief in getting the most critical horses safely off the property was now coupled with immense gratitude. Strangers, friends, acquaintances—so many people willing to lend a hand to horses in need.

Now, that is something to be thankful for! But that would mean seriously considering relocation for the rest.

"Tom, can you help me with some research?" I asked.

* * *

I yawned again, resting my head on Tom's chest, and said, "I hate to say it, but I think we need to get some sleep. I still don't feel totally prepared, but I'm going to be a zombie if I don't rest up."

He squeezed my shoulders. "Listen, we've done everything we can for tonight."

He was right. After obsessively researching for the past three hours, I'd learned so many things, like the rule of thumb in fire country that livestock should be immediately removed if a pre-evacuation order goes into effect. *Definitely not something you learn in law school!* And that we'd better start taking all this information and organizing it—lists with phone numbers, protocols, and procedures.

As I released those remaining anxious thoughts that always creep in late at night, when all is silent and still, and crossed over into the lovely state of presleep consciousness, I kept thinking the same thoughts, over and over: *the fire is too far away to threaten the ranch. It's just another Colorado wildfire . . .*

BCLU
FALL 1996

Warner Smith approached the stall as I tacked up my junior hunter, Gracie, for the ride.

"Couldn't help but admire the view," he commented suggestively, eyeing me from head to toe.

As one of the wealthiest men in Chester County and owner of several Grand Prix jumpers, Warner took liberties that few others could get away with, using his family's money to smooth over any inappropriate flirtation with the teenage girls at the barn.

If Warner had made that comment to Lacy or Morgan, they would have flirted back. Only a few years older than I, the two best friends had made a point to "educate" me in the ways of the hunter/jumper world I so desperately wanted to be a part of, providing unsolicited advice about fashion faux pas, making comments to me like "You can't afford it," and ensuring that I would be able to live the lifestyle I wanted. That is, if I was willing to do the "right" things with the wealthy, significantly older men.

"Emme, don't be a prude," Morgan had said the week before, when Warner first approached me.

Lacy backed up her friend. "Morgan's right. Warner is totally into you!"

Leering at me is more like it, I thought.

Morgan agreed. "You're lucky. You've got a rich guy interested in giving you everything you want! And all you've gotta do is give him what *he* wants? You will get to ride all the fanciest horses! Duh, no-brainer . . . because *you know* what brain Warner's thinking with!"

Lacy and Morgan looked at each other and started laughing, as if Morgan's comment was witty and smart.

But in some respects, they were right. I'd been part of that world long enough to know that unless you have unlimited funds, the best way to guarantee you can continue competing at a high level after you graduate and your parents stop paying for everything is to hook up with a wealthy man. So many of them are more than willing to drop their money on whatever horse a cute young girl might want, as long as said girl is willing to satisfy their other desires.

I saw it firsthand the year before, when Lacy got involved with Jeff Bartram. It was interesting to me that Lacy was so willing to get together with the middle-aged sponsor when she already came from an incredibly well-to-do family. As a matter of fact, I don't believe that Lacy's parents ever denied their youngest daughter anything. *Guess you can never have enough insurance to maintain the lifestyle.*

But try as I might, I just couldn't bring myself to do anything with—even kiss—the stocky and stubby Warner Smith. His breath smelled like mothballs, whiskey, or coffee, depending on the time of day. Not even my short theater stint in elementary school would allow me to tap into my inner actress and pretend I was remotely interested in this man who was almost double my age.

This was the inner battle I fought as a middle-class girl traveling in upper-class circles with stratospheric levels of entitlement. I so much wanted to fit in, but whenever I envisioned the price I needed to pay, I felt sick to my stomach.

In those moments, I would open my backpack and pull out the college brochure. *Screw these bitches' advice for how to make it in the hunter/jumper world. Laura agrees with me: a college degree and then a law degree from Villanova will give me the salary I need to remain in this world without sacrificing my standards. I could take out the necessary financial aid to do it.* Unlike Morgan and Lacy, Laura was level-headed and practical—and had become my best friend. Besides, she would never sleep her way to the top of anything!

Morgan's grating voice brought me back to reality. "Earth to Emme! I *said*, if you're not gonna go for it, may I? I really want to get the ride on Charisma. I need a better equitation horse for medal finals than the one I have.

It took a moment for her words to register. She laughed, as if I were the most naive person in the world. "C'mon, Emme. You know what I mean! Since Lacy already took Jeff . . ."

I forced a knowing laugh, as if teens dating older men were a totally normal thing to do. "Of course, Morgan. Who am I to get in the way of true love?" I quipped.

Morgan smiled and smoothed her crisp white shirt. "Thanks, Emme. I always knew you were cool." She moved toward Warner, twirling a lock of hair around her index finger and wiggling her hips as she walked.

With Morgan and Lacy distracted, I congratulated myself for not caving in but simultaneously hated myself for basking in Morgan's comment about being cool. I was also disappointed that I would not get the ride on Charisma. What riding him would have done for my last junior year!

Why do I feel such a need to fit in with them? If I looked up "mean girls" in the dictionary, their faces would be front and center.

Before I could get any more lost in my thoughts, my coach emerged from the other end of the barn, calling, "Ready, Emme? Time to ride!"

I looked at my mare—one of the more challenging horses I have ridden. Without the money tree the other girls had access to, my parents worked their asses off just to afford any horse, much less one that would be easy to ride. And although having my pick of any horse I wanted would have made riding easier, I knew that learning how to ride challenging horses put me light-years ahead of the competition. Being able to ride Gracie, an off-the-track thoroughbred, as well as Lacy rode her perfectly trained European import, Prestige, meant there was a deep connection between my thoughts and my horse's thoughts. I had won plenty with my off-the-track thoroughbred, but her breeding and talent would never compare to most of the other horses in the barn, no matter how much I loved or trusted her.

As I mounted Gracie and began to prepare for our warmup, I was finally able to forget about Morgan, Lacy, money, and creepy men. I loved this incredible outlet, where nothing else mattered except being one with the horse, the synergy that transpired as we hacked around, and the feeling of freedom. This is what riding always did for me—and why college and law school were going to be my ticket to many hunter/jumper years ahead. A fat paycheck to support this lifestyle seemed to be the most attainable route for someone like me—someone without a huge inheritance or trust fund.

CHAPTER 4

JUMP IN

OCTOBER 16, 2020

11:00 AM

Eerie. That's the only word that would describe the feeling I had when I drove under the C Lazy U Ranch archway a few hours earlier.

"I feel like I stayed up all night partying and smoking ten packs of cigarettes!" I joked to Molly. But underneath my jovial banter, I was worried. The smoke cloud over the pasture was growing thicker by the minute, obscuring the sun that fought to find an opening to shine through.

And now, sitting in the room with Jack and Tom, I knew it

was serious. Jack hated meetings more than he hated losing money, so the fact that he'd called for a critical meeting with Tom and me meant he was serious.

Jack's voice was droning on about horses and evacuated guests and volunteers and fire trucks and EMTs, but all I could think about were the horses. That beautiful mosaic of black and brown and white and speckled beauty, relaxing in the sunshine in West Meadow, clueless about the horror that could be lying in wait, threatening to overcome their home, their land. The horses were the reason I'd come. The reason I'd stayed.

I looked out the window at the billowing smoke that appeared to be so far away from the picturesque ranch. In fact, if I didn't know how dangerous the fire creating that smoke could be, I would have regarded the view as stunning. Instead, that smoke represented a threat to this magical place that began as a working ranch back in 1917, only to open its doors in 1919 as one of the first Western guest ranches—a place where affluent East Coast city slickers could play cowgirl and cowboy for a week or two at a dude ranch. I'm sure the staff back then never imagined that their ranch, with no heat, electricity, or running water, would one day boast a glass-floored spa over the river, a Zamboni pond for epic ice hockey games, and miles of cross-country trails running through this eighty-five-hundred-acre paradise.

Many of the reasons I fell in love with the ranch are similar to the reasons of many others who had the good fortune to visit C Lazy U. The moment I first drove down the long ranch driveway, I could feel the transformative energy that permeated every inch of the property, from the mountains and cowboy lifestyle to the friendships forged and staff who made everyone feel like family. People chose to visit again and again, year after year. When it was time to leave, they said it was worse than any romantic breakup. They cried on their last day, and their kids begged to stay longer. It was as if the ranch had a soul that spoke to anyone who visited, and the rest of the world faded into oblivion. C Lazy U allowed people an escape as they rejuvenated and rediscovered the joy in their hearts that might have been jaded or beaten down from the pressures of life. Some even decided to purchase ranch property and build second homes there.

And then, there's the horses. Where some dude ranches have run-of-the-mill horses that get the job done, C Lazy U takes pride in having only the best: horses that truly love their job, are well-trained, and are treated with the utmost respect. From the horses' glossy coats and glorious manes to their beautiful eyes that draw the rider into a wordless communion between human and animal, guests rightfully rave about the quality of the riding experience here and the horses themselves.

But now, some damn fire could threaten the ranch, the horses, our lives?

After a moment or two of shock that there was now an even stronger possibility that we would get an official pre-evacuation order, the logical and reasoning portion of my brain that had gotten me through all-nighters studying at Villanova kicked in. I did a quick assessment of the situation: more than two hundred horses, ten wranglers, eighty-two other staff, Tom, and me. Even though guests had been evacuated the day before, we still had close to three hundred other people and animals, all the tack and ranch equipment, and a ton of ranch artifacts, art, and property.

Tom noticed the look on my face as he sat across from me, then gave me the goofy smile that always made me laugh.

I love you, Tom, but it's just not working today. I felt the hot tears threaten to stream down my face, but I fought the urge, knowing I didn't have the luxury of time to cry. I refocused by staring intently toward the meadows, searching for my favorite tried-and-true guest horse, Fred. Of course, I loved them all, but Fred was the gelding that initially captured my heart, with his silly balding head and quirky personality. Every guest loved riding him and requested him year after year.

Jack's nasal voice interrupted my thoughts. "Emme, I know this is the last thing you want to hear, but we need to seriously consider how we're going to relocate all the horses."

I closed my eyes briefly and nodded. Once I was fairly confident I wasn't going to start bawling, I opened my eyes and looked Jack squarely in the eye.

"Of course. It's that bad?" I asked.

"It's not great. Fortunately, the Smiths and the Brightsides have offered their pastures, and they're only about ten miles south of here. And while I'm still hoping for the best, if we get that pre-evacuation call, you and I know it's go time."

3:30 PM

I was driving home to Granby to take a break from work and clear my head. My brain was in overdrive—not to mention the pounding headache from all the smoke. I needed perspective in making a decision that no head wrangler had ever faced at C Lazy U. One minute, I would feel fine, and the next, I'd be riddled with anxiety and doubt.

What if I'm putting the horses and staff in imminent danger? Even though we're not under pre-evacuation orders, one small shift in the winds could equal disaster.

I would never be able to forgive myself if something happened to the horses or staff, even though I had yet to know for sure that there would be any long-term effects on anyone's health from the smoke.

I picked up my phone and punched in the digits I knew so well. Then I smiled when I heard Russell's voice.

"How are you doing, Emme?"

The sound of Russell's relaxed drawl was comforting. "Thank you so much for taking my call, Russell. I could really use some advice."

As I described the wildfire forecast and evacuation plans, Russell waited patiently on the other end of the line, saying nothing. But I knew he was listening. If anything, he was the most patient, observant person I'd ever met. If anyone was going to know what to do, it would be him.

Once I got to the end of my spiel, I concluded with, "So, what do you think we should do?"

Russell laughed. "Emme, I love how much credit you give me, and yes, if this were about injured horses, ranch hand questions, or anything like that, I'd have decades of experience to back up my advice. But quite honestly, we never had a wildfire hit the ranch in any significant way."

Always humble and honest, Russell continued. "If I were to pretend to know how to advise you in this type of situation, I'd be fooling you and me that I know a lick about these things. Guess I'd never realized how lucky we were. Hell, the last time a wildfire impacted C Lazy U was back in '91, and the worst of it was canceling a few trail rides in the morning the first day or two that the smoke was at its worst. From what you're describing, this is unprecedented."

I nodded. Russell would never pretend to understand something he wasn't intimately knowledgeable about. It was another reason I implicitly trusted whatever he told me. But he was spot-on: C Lazy U had never seen the likes of something as dangerous as the East Troublesome Fire.

What he said next floored me, though.

Emme, you've got a better head on your shoulders

than anyone I've ever worked with. Better yet, you've got your priorities in order. Jack is taking care of the guests, and you're taking care of the horses—horses that have no idea how lucky they are to have someone with your heart making this decision. Whatever you decide is going to be in their best interests. I don't envy your position, though. And although I get bored with this retirement thing at times, it's at moments like this that I know I left at the right time. Your plan includes social media, emails, news stations . . . I would have no idea how to handle any of that! I'm an old-school cowboy, and this fire is calling for next-century skills. You're going to make the right decisions. I just know it. Trust yourself."

I sat with his words, allowing them to warm my heart and seep into my veins. Russell's belief in me was probably the only thing in the moment that prevented me from freaking out.

"Russell, you're too good to me, and you give me way too much credit! At the same time, I appreciate your honesty. I guess I was hoping you'd have some crazy experience and could tell me exactly what to do. But . . ."

"What is it, Emme?"

I fidgeted in the driver's seat as I drove. "Well, I know you're enjoying the retired life and all, but is there any chance you'd be willing to drive down the road and help load a couple hundred horses into trailers if we go under pre-evacuation?" I held my breath.

Russell laughed. "Thank you, Emme, for making me feel useful. I thought you'd never ask! Now, hopefully, it doesn't come to that. Sounds like the wind could shift and give the horses a break from the smoke. But if things don't go our way, you just give me the word, and I'm there."

I hung up the phone and pulled into my driveway. With the truck now in park, I looked out the back window of my Ford pickup. That warm feeling of reassurance from Russell disappeared, replaced by a pit in my stomach that dropped through the floor. What I saw was nothing short of terrifying: the billowing black smoke appeared to have grown even more dense, and the sky was now glowing red.

This was my first time witnessing a natural disaster—and it was horrifying.

Mother Earth and God are more powerful than I ever realized.

4:00 PM

It doesn't feel right staying here at home in Granby.

I walked back out to my car, turned the key in the ignition, and backed out of the driveway. *I need to seriously figure out how in the hell I am going to move two hundred horses.*

My vibrating phone interrupted my thoughts. It was Jack.

"Emme, bad news. We just got the pre-evacuation order."

4:15 PM

"Molly, I need you to get all the wranglers to the ranch ASAP," I said into my cell phone as I drove back to the ranch.

Molly gasped. "Is everything okay, Emme?"

Part of me wanted to be brutally honest and let her know how much I was freaking out in the moment. But then an image of Russell popped into my head. It was as if he were telepathically communicating with me: *Remember, people are like horses. They can read your energy.*

I willed myself to sound as calm as possible. "Everything is going to be fine, but only if we evacuate the horses, stat. I'm about three minutes away, but I need you to start making calls, okay?"

Her voice wavered, but she tried to sound strong. "Got it, Emme. I'll call them now!"

When I arrived at the ranch, I walked into Jack's office and dropped the updated fire plan on his desk. He thumbed through the pages, noting all the phone numbers and names.

"Emme, I'll start making the calls. I need you to take care of the horses."

I nodded and took a deep breath.

It's time.

BCLU

FEBRUARY 2009

I stood in our sleek, contemporary kitchen with all the latest appliances—and it was a mess. While I'd been at work all day, Reed (as usual) had not been. And if sitting around on his ass all day wasn't bad enough, he appeared to have spent any time off the couch opening every box and bag of snack food. Popcorn, chips, and Cheez-Its had spilled onto the counter.

Seeing that jumbled mess made something inside me snap. *Convenience or no, social connection or no, working for his dad or no, I can't follow through with this death-til-us-part union.* I had already been feeling resentful for months and had to come to terms with the fact that we actually had nothing in common. Reed thought horses were dumb. I felt the same way about most of his hobbies. Sure, we had fun going out with friends, but every time we arrived at a function, Reed would make a beeline to the bar (and hang there forever) while my girlfriends and I would sit around and bitch about our jobs, boyfriends, or both. *I don't care how much money he has. Feeling this miserable isn't worth it. I will find another way to afford to have horses in my life.*

I had been threatening to break things off with Reed for months, and I'm pretty sure nobody thought I'd go through with it. In fact, there were times even I didn't think I could call it off. But after my third summer trip to the ranch— precious time I gifted to myself each year to enjoy the horses and the land and to take time to reflect—I'd finally admitted to myself what we had. Actually, what we *didn't* have. And ever since I had returned to Philadelphia after a couple of weeks of business travel, I couldn't unknow what was true in my heart.

So that day, after mowing through mile-high stacks of briefs and countless meetings with difficult clients, the sight of Reed sitting in the living room doing nothing, as usual, except sipping on a pretentious glass of Veuve Clicquot, made it clear that I couldn't handle another second of it.

Grabbing a garbage bag, I swept everything off the counter and into the bag. Along with the snacks, I swiped empty wineglasses, bottles, and even a candle or two. As the bottles, glasses, and candles shattered, Reed turned his head toward the kitchen.

"Babe. What are you doing?"

The completely clueless and relaxed expression on his face gave me the urge to dump the bag of trash on his head. Instead, I tied a knot and threw the bag to the floor, making crushed glass noises that were even louder on the hard surface.

"What am I doing? What am I *doing*? *WHAT AM I DOING?*" I laughed maniacally, as if I had finally lost my mind, Stephen-King-Red-Rum style.

That got his attention. The half-closed eyelids shot open, and the slumped shoulders stood at attention, as if waiting for marching orders.

"I'll tell you what I'm doing. Leaving!" By now, I was screaming and crying all at once. Reed stood up and walked over to me, making a half-hearted attempt to put his arms around me. I shoved him away.

"Stop, Reed. It's over. This—" I swept my arms in a large circle, pointing at the kitchen, then the hallway, then the living room. "This. Is. Over." I yanked a paper towel from the stainless-steel rack and wiped my eyes.

Suddenly feeling calm, I lowered my voice to a whisper, so soft that Reed leaned in to hear my words.

"Reed, *we* are over."

CHAPTER 5

HEATING UP

OCTOBER 16, 2020

5:00 PM

I'm glad my fear that we might actually need to cut the fence and jingle the horses to safety gave me the idea of keeping so many of our jingle horses and lead mares in the corrals.

As soon as I parked my truck, I raced over to the corral and headed toward my jingle pony. Dually was an ex-rodeo horse, fast and responsive whenever I needed him to switch into fifth gear. The bond and trust I had with him were second to none.

At the sound of my shrill, scared voice, Dually looked up and immediately began walking toward me. I haltered him and led him to the lower barn, where all my tack was stored.

Within two minutes, Dually was tacked up. Allison and Lexi appeared with their jingle horses, and I saw more wranglers filing into the corral. Everyone had gotten back to the ranch in record time. I mounted Dually and rode alongside Lexi and Allison out over the Willow Creek toward East Meadow, where most of the horses were pastured.

"Girls!" I called. "We need to get them in as fast as possible, no matter what!"

Allison nodded, indicating that she understood that this fire had the potential to impact our lives. Lexi simply gave me a noncommittal thumbs-up—and that's when I gave the jingle call. The horses must have sensed something was wrong, because the moment I gave the jingle call, they ran toward the gate faster than I'd ever seen them move. Their lean bodies galloped effortlessly, their manes whipping in the strong wind as their glossy coats stood in stark contrast against the red-orange sky that continued to rain down ash. Terrified, I glanced at Dually's mane, which was now filled with white specks.

Thank God they're cooperating! The last thing I need is to chase them around the pasture.

Despite the horses' cooperation, my hands shook as I opened the latch on the gate. The other wranglers held the horses in place while Dually and I opened the double gate for the herd to go through. Once the gate was open, I quickly jumped out in front and led the herd in from the pasture to the corrals. Once the last horse had run into the corral, I jumped off Dually and dialed Russell's number. I cursed my trembling hands as it took me three tries to dial it correctly.

"Hello?" he said.

I forced myself to breathe deeply so I wouldn't burst into tears. "Hey, Russell . . . I guess you know what this means?"

"They made the pre-evacuation call?"

I nodded, even though I knew he couldn't see me. "You got it. I really could use your help. All these people are asking me for direction, and I still don't know if our plan will actually work."

Russell waited until I was finished speaking before he responded. "You've got this, kid. You're gonna be great. Just trust your instincts, and I'll be there soon."

I pressed the red icon on my phone to end the call and took a moment to breathe.

What the hell, Russell? You think I've got this? Me?

As much as I wanted nothing more than to hand the reins over to Russell, I knew he must have been seeing something in me that I couldn't see. But with Russell's spot-on instincts in every other situation, I had to trust that if he said I could handle it . . . Well, then maybe I could. *Plus,* I reminded myself, *you're lucky to have wranglers like Jessica and Kai, who extended their contracts through October.* I shuddered to think what this ordeal would be like with newbies.

With that little pep talk, I headed to the lower barn to untack Dually. I buried my face in his warm neck and took a few deep breaths, trying to push away the anxiety attack I so badly wanted to have. I stepped back, gave Dually a couple of treats, turned him into the corrals, then headed toward the wrangling crew, who were all waiting patiently for me in the historic upper barn that had been in existence since 1921. As I headed toward the crew, I saw Dually hook back up with Mungo, a giant half-draft paint horse that was his best buddy.

Fake it til you make it, Em.

I did my best to look confident as I directed the team.

"Lexi and Kyra, you're in charge of loading the horses onto the trailers. Russell can help you when he arrives." The two girls nodded, and I knew that with Russell's horse-whispering skills, Lexi and Kyra would have no problem.

"Joey, I need you to go hook up our large stock trailer and be ready to haul horses." Joey gave me a thumbs-up and jogged toward the haul truck.

"Jessica, you keep track of which horses are getting onto which trailer. Nicole and Kai, please help the kids' counselors halter the other groups over there. Allison, I need you to organize the catching. And Molly, you can help me halter this group over here. Oh, and team?"

Everyone grew silent, seeming to sense that what I was going to say next was important. "We need to make sure we keep the horses with their friends! It'll be easier to load them that way."

I moved toward Gypsy and her group of friends, and everyone else began their assigned tasks.

Frantic yet focused, we all seemed to understand how critical it would be to have all the horses ready for the trailers when they arrived. I kept reminding myself that every second would count as we loaded Joey's trailer.

At first, I was so busy with Joey's trailer that I didn't immediately notice the spectacular sight that was in progress: within a mere twenty minutes, and with everyone moving in the right direction, a line of approximately one hundred trailers of all shapes and sizes was snaking down the dirt road. To see this ranch community come together in a pinch filled my heart with gratitude. *You would never see people come together like this back home!*

I said another silent prayer of thanks that Jack had handled all those phone calls and details. *There's no way I could be taking care of the horses while trying to rustle up all these volunteers to help move them.*

My strategy seemed to be both effective and efficient: keep the horses in small herds that have their unspoken friendships and subgroups with leaders—just like in high school, where the jocks follow the quarterback around, and the band kids look up to the drum major. The herd dynamics were eerily similar to my high school days. In this case, Gypsy was a lead mare, and with her best friend, Janet, by her side, she made sure their little subgroup of five geldings quickly followed them wherever they went.

No sooner had Gypsy's trailer driven off than the horrifying thought hit me: *How are we transporting the Clydesdales and Belgians?* These animals were far too big for a typical-sized trailer. I realized our ranch neighbors had fortunately left no stone unturned as I watched a semitruck approach with one of the largest trailers I'd ever seen. When the mammoth trailer pulled up, we readied our big guys for loading.

Big Fred was a Belgian well over twenty hands tall that had been gifted to the ranch many years back with his partner and best friend, Big Mike, to pull our sleigh during the winter. Fred had a tendency to get triggered in high-anxiety situations or when people applied too much pressure. I watched Russell take his lead rope from one of the wranglers and immediately calm Fred down as he followed Big Mike onto the trailer that was large enough to accommodate a horse of Fred's size. Watching these two big boys load, I took a moment to remember how those two had pulled Santa's sleigh last Christmas while Santa handed out gifts to all the kids on the ranch—a wonderful memory that I prayed we would be able to see again.

Hulk, another draft horse, was next. The name belied his current condition: ill and weak. He had been sick for the past month with an immunodeficiency that we had been trying to treat with little success. I held my breath as he lumbered onto the trailer, and I exhaled when he took his last step inside.

As I turned away, I heard Molly scream. "Omigod, Hulk!"

He must have somehow lost his balance because when I turned back to look, he was on his knees, struggling to lift his massive body upright. For a split second, the horrific thought crossed my mind: *Could this be it for him? Will we need to euthanize him here? Now? He's too weak to even walk. Shit, shit, shit . . .*

The sadness in knowing that this stupid fire might force me to euthanize one of these incredible animals was more than I would be able to handle. I cursed to myself and started preparing myself for the worst-case scenario.

Thankfully, with the help of several ranch hands and volunteers who snapped into action when they heard Molly's cry for help, Hulk managed to right himself and lift his giant body into the trailer. Yet again, I fought back tears—but this time, they were tears of gratitude that Hulk was such a fighter.

Hulk, you badass! You're not done fighting yet.

As the girls haltered and loaded the horses, I directed what horses would go onto which trailers. Meanwhile, Kai and Jessica crossed off each horse's name and snapped pictures of license plates with their iPhones as they loaded to keep track of what horses went on each trailer in the caravan.

I glanced over at the rest of the girls, who were working their tails off, and my self-doubt was replaced by a sense of wonder. Their dedication and ability to keep their emotions in check was nothing short of amazing. They had clearly pushed their typical fears aside, knowing that remaining in control would make or break this operation. And I couldn't believe I was the one orchestrating this mass exodus.

Not quite like Moses in the desert, but wow. I somehow am managing to not look like an insecure freak and am actually pulling this off without losing the respect of my whole crew and the entire town of Granby.

Watching these powerful animals and wranglers all moving in a synchronized rhythm was a sight to behold— but there was no time to pause.

As the winds raged and the smoke grew heavier, I reminded myself to focus on one thing and one thing only: the horses. I couldn't have been prouder of them. They were marching onto the strange, dark trailers as if they did this every day. Some of the volunteers turned on the flashlights on their phones, especially as they coaxed some of the groups into completely dark cattle trailers.

Getting the horses into the trailers was no small feat, considering some of them had never stepped foot off the ranch—making this plan a testament to the horsemanship that had been prevalent at C Lazy U for years. The horses intuitively understood that we were all there to help them, and they trusted us without question.

Out of the one hundred and ninety-two horses we loaded that night, only five put up a fight. But in their defense, these were the ones that were going into a trailer for the very first time—and their trailers were completely pitch dark.

Storm was by far the most resistant, rejecting every human who tried to cajole her onto the trailer. I could tell that with each person who attempted to load her, Storm's trust was diminishing by the second—and I knew we had no other choice but to sedate her. Out of desperation and a lack of time, I directed Molly to give her a sedative. It wasn't how I normally liked to do things, but it was the only safe solution when every second counted.

Damn. I failed Storm. When this is all over, I need to spend some extra time with her. Get to know her better. Rebuild her trust in humans.

Meanwhile, the ranch hands were busy scurrying around, clearing out the barn and securing other areas of the property—a heartwarming sight to see during such a trying time. Two of the hands loaded more than two hundred saddles, bridles, blankets, harnesses, ropes, and any other potentially useful tack they could find into a snowmobile trailer that a volunteer had cleverly decided to bring for this very purpose, along with any open-bed truck they could find. Jack and Tom continued directing traffic, and people I'd never met before kept approaching to ask what they could do to help.

I turned to one of the volunteers with tears in my eyes. "Can I just tell you how grateful we are for your help? In fact, everyone's help?"

A woman, gray-haired and probably in her sixties, nodded, tears in her eyes as well. "I know. It's unbelievable, but we all know how much y'all love this ranch. And I don't just mean you." She gestured to the C Lazy U staff, scrambling and working. "I always knew this was a special place. It's been part of our community for a long time. A staple of historic Grand County."

I sniffed and wiped my eyes as Allison approached, ready for more.

"Allison, I need you to head to the first evacuation ranch to make sure the unloading goes well."

Her eyes danced, as she was clearly excited to be given an even bigger responsibility. "You got it!"

She jogged toward her truck while I turned back to my list. One hundred of the horses were going to a neighboring ranch with a large pasture about ten miles down the road, and the other ninety-two would go to a smaller neighboring pasture. The plan would require us to move the herd in the morning so all the horses would be in the same two-hundred-and-fifty-acre pasture, but there was no way to access it at night, so these two pastures would have to suffice for now.

I'll worry about moving the horses around tomorrow.

About thirty minutes later, my phone vibrated, and I pulled it out of my pocket. "Allison, everything okay?" I asked.

She sounded out of breath. "Yes, everything's okay—at least for now. But when I got here, some of the horses got spooked because they couldn't find their friends right away. Lee ran through the barbed wire trying to find Gypsy and actually busted through the fence when he caught sight of her. Luckily, I think the wounds are superficial; as soon as he got back with Gypsy, he didn't seem to have a care in the world. We will need to check on him in the morning. It's too dark to see anything clearly."

I winced at the thought of Lee, a beautiful brown-and-white paint gelding, getting cut and slashed with barbed wire. Shuddering at the thought of how fearful he must've felt, I took another deep breath, reminding myself that everyone was okay.

"All right, thanks for the update. But just to be safe, call Dr. Hecksher, and ask her to check Lee out tomorrow."

"Will do, Emme. Bye!" Allison's voice sounded more relaxed.

She was probably worried that I would be upset. But none of this was her fault. I mean, who can be angry with some unexpected glitches in a chaotic situation like this? None of us have ever experienced anything like it in our lives!

9:00 PM

As the last horse stepped onto a trailer, my stomach relaxed for the first time in hours. All the worry about horses getting lost, someone making off with one of our nicer quarter horses, a horse getting sick, and just the general fear of uprooting these beautiful creatures from their home began to subside.

"Hey, guys?" I motioned for silence, and everyone paused with a collective look of dread on their faces. *They must think I am going to give them more work.*

I smiled. "I think it's time to head over to the lodge bar and grab ourselves a drink or two. What do you think?"

Everyone smiled, and I heard a few people say, "Hell yeah," as I walked toward the lodge bar to join the crew for a celebratory whiskey.

10:00 PM

The bartender walked over to Russell, Tom, and me with a tray of shots. "That guy over there said congratulations," he told us.

We turned toward a table in the corner, where Jack was sitting alone. He raised his shot glass and winked. I felt giddy with a combination of relief and happiness from the outpouring of love our community had demonstrated over the past few hours.

Tom bellowed, "Jack, get over here and drink with us!"

Jack sauntered over to the bar, and we clinked glasses as we tilted our heads back, downing Fireball. After Jack finished his shot, he said, "I've got to hand it to all of you. I didn't think we could pull it off, but we did, thanks to you . . . and you . . . and you." Jack took turns nodding at me, Russell, Tom, and the rest of the crew.

Jack never compliments anyone. Goes to show how monumental this moment is!

Jack set his shot glass on the bar and made eye contact with the bartender, making a clockwise motion with his hand to get another round for the group.

Then he turned back to us. "So, the fire is still over ten miles away, which means we don't have any risk of the ranch being in danger at the moment. However, we still need to be prepared for the worst-case scenario—the fire hopping the mountain and crossing the road."

I contemplated what that would mean. Removing all the fancy artwork and any other items of value from the ranch? *That would take hours!*

Russell shook his head with disbelief. "With all due respect, Jack, I think the chances of that happening are slim to none."

Jack remained somber. "I agree, Russell. But if this fire has been predictable in any way, it's been its unpredictability that we can count on! I'm simply exercising an extreme abundance of caution, which is why I brought in a few more volunteers to help us remove some more things from the ranch tomorrow—just in case."

I raised my eyebrows and assessed which ranch hands were missing from the lodge and still working. Jack laughed.

"Emme, not *our* team. I wouldn't ask them to put in overtime after what they did today. No, there were some more volunteers who couldn't make it in time to trailer the horses but were more than willing to use their vehicles for some artwork and furniture."

Tom, ever the optimist, spoke next. "Good idea, Jack! Let's hope we were simply overcautious on that one, but I think it was smart. And now, with everything taken care of for the night, let's enjoy what's left of the evening. I think we all deserve it!"

Russell gave Jack a hearty slap on the back in agreement, and the men started talking sports as if to distract themselves from the horror of the recent events.

"Woo-hoo, girls! We did it!" Kyra's voice rose above the din of clanking glassware and the hum of celebratory conversations. I looked toward the other end of the bar, where a few of the girls raised shot glasses of tequila with gratitude in the direction of a local volunteer who must've known how momentous this evening had been and paid for a round for the entire staff.

Molly squeezed her eyes shut after downing the alcohol, while Kyra, who clearly had an affinity for tequila, slammed her glass down and motioned to the bartender that they were ready for another round.

Meanwhile, I sat silent, trying to brush aside the worried feeling in my gut. *C'mon, Emme. The worst is behind us. Stop being so paranoid! The horses are safe!* But the feeling wouldn't go away—not after the second shot, and not even as I slipped into bed later that evening at home.

Tom must have sensed my worry because he grabbed my hand and squeezed it.

"Emme, everything is going to be okay. Promise! Now, get some sleep." He pulled me in close, and I soon heard the snoring that let me know he was already in dreamland.

I hope Tom is right about this one.

BCLU

MAY 2011

I swiped left again. And again.

Chris is cute! Green flag. Severely allergic to "most animals"? Red flag. I scrolled again. *Adam just made partner at his law firm! Green flag. Seems to only like taking selfies and flexing without his shirt on. Must be vain? Red flag.*

Frustrated with every so-called match on Match.com, I put my phone down and looked out the window of the plane as it taxied toward the terminal. Just imagining what it would feel like to drive up to C Lazy U in a couple of hours helped any anxiety melt away.

I thought back to how I somehow made this possible, especially without the big paycheck from Krinsky and Sheirburg. Soon after I called off the engagement that fateful day over two years earlier (and by default called off my career through Reed's dad), I jumped ship and joined

Levin and Marple, a lower-paying but highly regarded firm in Philly that was situated right next door to Laura's new digs at Rittenhouse One.

I smiled at the memory of Laura dancing around the day she found out she was finally going to be able to rent there: the woman's Maltese had suddenly passed away, and now nothing was holding the elderly tenant back from vacating the unit Laura had so desperately wanted to lease for almost two years.

"I know it's kind of wrong that I'm celebrating . . . poor little dog! But I'm just *so* happy! You know how long I waited for that woman to make the move to Rittenhouse Two!" Laura had stopped dancing for a moment and looked me in the eye. "Emme, promise you'll visit often! You can spend the night in the guest bedroom."

I'd nodded as a thought formed in my mind. "Laura, I have an idea . . ."

I told her about Levin and Marple's job offer and where the office was located. As soon as she heard the name, she instantly understood. "Em, your work is literally next door! Live with me—please! It'll be like a girl's night, twenty-four/ seven!"

The memories continued, filling me with a rush of gratitude toward Laura as I stood up to exit the plane, knowing I couldn't have taken the pay cut I did when I left Reed— and my job with his dad—and still manage to save money to move out West. The rent she had charged me was so ridiculously cheap that I was able to save enough to cover my expenses for months.

The day Laura asked me to move in with her was the same day I started putting my plan into motion: pass the Colorado bar, give thirty days' notice at Levin and Marple, and set up an interview with Russell for a wrangler job at C Lazy U. Work as a wrangler for six months and then find a real job.

The entire plan took almost two years, but everything fell into place, piece by piece, despite friends and family questioning my sanity while I kept convincing them that not only was my mental state intact, but I was happier than I had been in years. Even the stress of packing up my life and leaving it behind in a storage unit in Ridley Park couldn't dim my spirits. Instead of my typical tendency to overpack, I knew that moving into a bunkhouse with twelve other girls would afford me only the bare necessities.

Leaving a six-figure salary behind for the dream of working on a dude ranch for a fraction of that money might have seemed absurd to most. But to me, the feeling of freedom—knowing I'd basically told the world to fuck off—was one of the most empowering moments in my life. I wouldn't have traded this for the world! As that credit card company advertisement touts, this moment was *priceless*.

Still . . .

I was riddled with self-doubt and panic every time I thought about my massive law school loans and how I was going to pay them. I had saved up enough to give myself six months for this venture—and to say I would be screwed if I couldn't find another law firm in Denver that would want to hire me would be an understatement!

But I couldn't think about it because every time I did, my plan felt more and more like a dumb idea. *It's going to be okay!* These were the words I kept telling myself because I simply had to keep the faith and hope that all those years of school would allow me to secure another job. No one walked away from a law career—at least, not when they had as much student loan debt as I did! But I was drowning and needed to be able to breathe again. This break was exactly what I needed.

So now, there I was, just hours away from the opportunity to play cowgirl for a few months. Of course, at some point, I would need to look for a "real" job with a firm in Denver. *But first, it's time to enjoy life for a bit and ride some horses!*

* * *

"Hi, I'm Emme." I shook hands with the tall, rugged-looking yet muscular stranger who had introduced himself as Tom.

"What brings you to C Lazy U?" Tom smiled, and I felt my heart jump when I looked into his blue eyes. Instantly, I felt this strange yet comforting connection with him, like I was coming home for the first time.

Fearing I would stumble over my words, I silently chastised

myself. *C'mon, Em. Get your shit together and pretend you meet guys this good-looking all the time. Poise and grace.*

I cleared my throat and took a deep breath. "I'm going to be working as a wrangler for the summer season, so I have a meeting set up with, Russell, uh . . ." my voice trailed off as I scrambled to remember his last name.

Tom smiled, clearly unaware of my nerves. "Oh, so *you're* the one! For some reason, I thought EM were initials on Russell's calendar and you were going to be a guy." He laughed. "*That* couldn't be further from the truth."

Is he flirting or just being friendly? I couldn't be sure, but before I could say anything else, the man who was a dead ringer for the Marlboro Man cowboy walked through the door. No matter how many times I had seen him over the years, Russell's presence always felt larger than life to me.

"Emme Mueller?" he drawled, his voice smooth and sweet as molasses syrup.

"Yes, sir." I stood up straight and extended my hand. "It's good to see you again, Mr. . . ."

"Just call me Russell, Emme! That's what you've always called me, so why should that change now? We don't stand on ceremony here or think too highly of ourselves either. If we had our head in the clouds, we'd float away in the thin mountain air." He smiled and gestured toward Tom. "I see you met our mountain bike and hiking guide, Tom Trego."

This introduction gave me another opportunity to gaze

into the ice-blue eyes that seemed to be melting my heart. "Yes, I did."

Russell continued. "Tom here used to be an East Coaster like yourself, but once he got out here, his summer 'break' lasted a *little* longer than expected . . ." Russell trailed off, giving Tom the opportunity to tell his own story.

Tom took the cue. "Russell's right. Originally, I worked crazy eighty-hour weeks for a tech start-up in New Jersey, but the cubicle life wasn't for me. Wasn't a big fan of the stuffed-shirt crowd either."

I could easily picture him in Vineyard Vines, yet his T-shirt and Mountain Khakis shorts more aptly suited the laid-back personality he exuded.

The mountain guide look is way sexier too.

Tom laughed as if recalling a memory. "Of course, my family can't understand why I don't want to use my MBA for some Fortune 500, but they've never gotten hooked on mountain biking, skiing, and climbing these giant mountains like I have. I mean, the privacy of being able to ride hundreds of miles without anyone bothering me? It's like heaven!" He paused as if gauging my interest level before continuing. "Anyway, the plan was to take a break from the rat race, y'know? I planned to hang here for a few months, and then make my way down to Moab to keep living the dream. But there's just something about this place that drew me in. To be honest, I'm *really* glad I stayed put in Colorado."

Once again, I wondered if he might be flirting or just pitching C Lazy U to make it sound appealing for an interviewee. *Maybe he's just a friendly guy with everyone?*

Russell interrupted my racing thoughts. "Well, enough about us! Let's go back to my office so I can make sure this successful lawyer from Philadelphia with her fancy designer luggage really wants to be a wrangler."

He pointed toward a room at the back of the building, and I followed him, crossing my fingers for good luck—good luck that I'd not only convince Russell I wasn't going to be the weak-willed, pretentious, and whiny pain-in-the-ass guest he seemed to think I was going to be but that I also might see Tom again. Soon.

* * *

As I signed the seasonal wrangler contract, my hands shook with a combination of giddy anticipation that *Yes, I'm really doing this!* Along with a nervous *What the hell am I doing? From six figures to six dollars an hour after taxes.*

Despite my nerves, that *knowing* deep inside let me know I was doing the right thing. As I finished signing my name, a sense of peace and calm filled my entire body, confirming that everything had been worth it: the broken engagement, killer work hours, constant fighting to be the best and brightest, staying home Friday nights to save some money when everyone else was headed out to Chickie's &

Pete's or Talula's Garden or The Library Bar, and studying once again for another bar exam to be able to practice in the Rocky Mountain State. It was worth the sacrifice to be here, in this perfect place, to finally do what I loved most: ride. And I could do it without anyone expecting anything of me.

Besides, this gig won't last forever. After six months or so, I can look for another law firm to join.

Practically floating out of Russell's office and the building, I almost didn't see Tom sitting on the porch as I exited.

"Emme?"

He was sitting on an old rocking chair, the sun catching his hair's natural blond highlights.

"Yes?"

"Um, I know we just met, but would you like to meet for dinner this evening?"

Before I could respond, he added, "I know you're new to the area. So I could fill you in on all the great local spots so you don't fall into the overpriced tourist traps. Of course, there's not much around here, but we could meet up in Granby."

I smiled. *I'm pretty sure this is a date and not just a welcome wagon invitation.*

"I'd love to. What time?"

CHAPTER 6

WELCOME TO
THE JINGLE

OCTOBER 17, 2020
6:30 AM

I watched in amazement as the wranglers and ranch hands scarfed down the Java Lava breakfast and blueberry muffins I had hastily arranged on the kitchen table. Tom had already left about an hour earlier to continue securing the ranch with the ranch hands and maintenance team and assist the fire department by cutting down as many trees and branches from around the cabins as possible.

As I surveyed the room and massaged my throbbing temples, I reminded myself not to do shots on an empty stomach ever again. I watched the girls huddle over Kyra's phone, laughing at some TikTok video, while Allison and Jessica high-fived and reminisced about the events of the previous day in play-by-play detail. The mood in the room was light and slightly euphoric, as if we had all enjoyed some of the Rocky Mountain State's legal weed. The giggling and laughing were a clear indication that the collective sleep deprivation had put everyone in a silly state of near delirium.

Turning away from the group, I consulted my to-do list: move the horses into one pasture from the Smith and Brightside ranches to a pasture we could call home until we were able to go back to the ranch. Ms. Smith had mentioned that there was a large back pasture that could work, and I was hoping this would solve that problem. The sooner we could get the herd back together, the easier feeding and caring for them would be.

Next, we needed to check on all the horses and make sure no one sustained any injuries during the chaotic trailering from the night before. We also needed to get senior grain, supplements, and medication for the older ones. Since it was late October, we also needed an abundance of hay to feed the horses due to the lack of grass; with almost two hundred horses, they would eat the Smith pasture down to the dirt in no time.

I clapped my hands a few times to get everyone's attention. "So, I've got some good news, ladies! Sounds like the winds have shifted, and the smoke isn't as bad as we anticipated. The firefighters seem to have the fire somewhat under control today, with more fire lines being cut. But . . ."

I paused, knowing if I minimized the fire too much, they might let down their guard more than they should.

"Nothing about this fire has been predictable, so we need to be ready for all possible scenarios. I'm going to head over to the Smith ranch and meet with their foreman. Hopefully, we can determine the best location for the horses to live until we can return home."

I pushed the nagging worry to the back of my mind: *If you can't find a place, Emme, you have no backup plan.* Although I had been hoping the evacuation would only last a few days, I was finally coming to terms with the fact that returning to the ranch might not be happening anytime soon, so it was critical to find a more suitable semipermanent pasture for the horses.

Before they could get distracted by their phones again, I divided the girls into teams and gave them their assignments for the day. They loaded up their cars and trucks with all the tack, chinks, and as many provisions as they could think of, knowing the horses might need supplies in their new "homes."

Senior feed for older horses? Check. Dr. Hecksher on call? Check. Inspecting the horses for injuries? Check.

Despite their night out, the girls were obviously raring to

go, running on a combination of sleep deprivation, adrenaline, euphoria, and caffeine.

Once everyone left our house, I threw out the used paper plates and napkins, wiped down the table, and grabbed my keys. *The Smith ranch will be perfect. Two hundred and fifty acres of land under the watchful eye of Ms. Smith.*

The moment I pulled up to the ranch and caught sight of the matriarch, Ms. Hattie Smith, I knew we were in good hands. I could tell that behind her slight, somewhat wispy frame, which looked so tiny against the backdrop of the looming farmhouse, was a fiery spirit that was all cowgirl and cattle.

I climbed the porch steps and felt the wooden planks of the wraparound porch creak under my feet. Hattie rushed over to me and enveloped me in a bear hug.

"Emme, darlin'! How are you holding up?"

For a moment, I teared up. Except for Tom, it was the first time anyone had asked how *I* was feeling. But I resisted the temptation to soften and instead took a deep breath and reminded myself that there would be time to process everything later.

"Thank you for asking, Hattie. But I'm doing okay, all things considered. I just want to make sure the horses have a real 'home' for as long as this takes. If that makes sense?"

Hattie nodded. "Of course that makes sense! So, to put your mind at ease, let me introduce you to Beau, my head foreman. He'll give you the grand tour."

Beau squinted and eyed me up, as if to calculate how

much of an annoyance I would create by interrupting his cattle operation. His cowboys had been trickling in at the same time the girls arrived, and I prayed that the Smith cowboys' testosterone wouldn't distract some of my boy-crazy girls. Unfortunately, I knew the girls too well and cringed as I watched Kyra sidle up next to a particularly good-looking blond cowboy and strike up a conversation. I couldn't make out the words, but considering Kyra's seductive body language, she wasn't talking about the horses.

Beau snorted in response to Kyra's flagrant flirtation, and he turned to me. "Y'know, not only are you pulling me away from my business, but your, ahh, *girls*," he drawled with disdain, "appear to be more interested in my boys than rescuing any horses. I mean, do these young ladies even know how to ride? Ride a horse, that is. Clearly, they know how to ride other things." He chuckled menacingly.

I felt my face flush with anger. *Damn you, Kyra! Now I've got to defend you because you've got to act like some helpless thing the second a hot guy shows up.* But my anger toward Beau's ignorant macho act was much stronger than my irritation with Kyra.

"With all due respect, *Beau*." I attempted to spit out his name with the same nasty tone he directed at my girls. "Not only can these ladies ride horses, but they can ride circles around any cow *boy*." I smiled inwardly, purposely separating the two words and emphasizing the word *boy* to get under Beau's skin.

It worked. For a moment, he seemed surprised—and even a bit impressed—that I'd stood up to his swaggering attitude and no-bullshit façade.

He softened his voice slightly. "Well, we'll see about their riding skills. Time will tell. But enough of this chitchat. Lemme give you the tour."

As Beau and Hattie drove me around in their four-wheel-drive Jeep, I knew this back pasture was the perfect fit. The abundant aspen trees would protect the horses from any adverse weather, while the road to get to the pasture was easily accessible. Not only that, but there was a small stream running through the pasture, providing a natural water source. Even better, the jingle from the front corral, where the horses were currently located, to this back pasture did not seem that complicated. It was less than a mile, and we only had to make two turns.

Beau's voice interrupted my thoughts. "Now, I know the pasture doesn't seem that far, but you need to be on guard at all times, Emme. There are a few turns where things could go terribly wrong if you lose any of the herd. There are also some gnarly gopher holes and some old barbed wire fence lines. But don't worry too much about it—I'll make sure my boys are there to be on the lookout."

I resisted the urge to argue with Beau that my girls didn't need extra help, yet I trusted his assessment of the terrain and knew I couldn't let my ego get in the way of his advice if it meant keeping the horses safe. *But these horses—and*

the girls—are so good that I know they're going to get it right!
Despite my personal insecurities, I had extreme confidence
when it came to my horses and team of wranglers.

Hattie nodded, confirming Beau's warning. "I know the fire
is still at a distance, about seven miles away. The firefighters
are putting up fire lines, trying to keep it contained to the
national forest area. But it's burning through the deadfall,
and that's the challenge."

Everything Hattie and Beau said was true. But for once, I
was feeling relatively calm. Maybe it was the Indian summer
day that seemed less smoky. Perhaps it was the realization
that the winds had stopped—another good sign that the fire
could be kept under control. Or maybe the knowledge that
the fire was miles away gave me a false sense of security.
Or the fact that I hadn't slept the night before. Whatever
the reason, I felt supremely optimistic. And thank God I
did, because little did I know that this was going to be the
wildest ride of my life!

* * *

The wranglers sat on their assigned horses, ready to go.
Even though they didn't know the area as well as Beau made
it sound, the young cowboys from the Smith ranch tried to
look like they knew what they were doing in an attempt
to impress the pretty wrangler girls. I covered my mouth
and giggled as I watched the girls saddle up, knowing they

would soon put those cowboys to shame as they rode the crap out of their horses.

My phone buzzed. It was Molly. She called to tell me that Echo had hit her head in the trailer the night before, and I felt my stomach drop.

"You can see her skull through all the dried blood, Emme!" Molly's voice caught, and I knew she was trying her best not to cry.

"Molly, take a breath." I paused for a moment, knowing she wouldn't be paying any attention to my words until she calmed down.

"Okay . . ." Molly's voice still shook, but she sounded less panicked.

Although I was envisioning Echo's bloody head and feeling rather frantic myself, I knew I needed to maintain my composure—for everyone's sake. "Let's call Dr. Hecksher and see if she can come over and put some sutures in her."

"Mm-hmm," Molly replied, but I could tell she hadn't really heard a word I said.

"In the meantime, I just need you to check Echo's vitals, okay?"

Molly sniffled. "I already did that, and her vitals look good. I called Dr. Hecksher already too. She's here now."

I breathed a sigh of relief. *That's impressive. Molly had the presence of mind to take the vitals and call the vet. Her emotions probably didn't even kick in until she called me.*

"That's great, Molly!" I said. "Way to work under pressure! Can you put her on the line?"

All I could hear were scratchy sounds for a moment, and then the cool voice of Dr. Hecksher filled my ears. "Emme?"

"How's Echo?"

"She's fine, Emme. Molly here is a little shook up, but your horse is just fine. I stitched her up, and I'm confident she will be okay. We'll put her on antibiotics for seven days just to make sure we don't have an infection."

I exhaled, instantly feeling better as I heard the experienced vet's soothing voice.

I gave a thumbs-up to Hattie, who had seen the look on my face and edged closer to my phone, which I had turned to speaker mode so she could listen in. She smiled and gave a thumbs-up in return.

"Echo should be fine," I said. "We just need to get her cleaned up! Thank God. I don't think I can take many more curveballs."

Hattie patted my shoulder. "You're doin' just fine, sweetheart. But I'm glad the old girl's going to be okay." She looked at the rest of the girls, who were waiting for further direction. "Now what?"

I turned back to the rest of the group, relieved that at least one crisis had been averted. "Okay, everyone. You've all been assigned a spot, so everyone is either riding a horse in a group or riding a lead mare. And remember, we've got blockers, flankers, leaders, and pushers, so your job is to make sure the horses stay together and get to the pasture!" I paused. "Oh, and one more thing. Don't add any unnecessary pressure or chase the horses if they get away from us."

The sea of nodding heads indicated they were paying attention.

Jessica rode Wilma, who was one of the most dominant mares (and was worshiped by a gaggle of geldings), while Lexi rode Gypsy and Allison rode Pearl. I had made this assignment carefully, knowing we could control the first large group of horses because they would follow these particular mares. Jessica and Lexi were going to lead the herd to the pasture, while Allison was going to control the herd's speed by pushing from behind.

I was riding Phil, a responsive quarter horse that was a guest favorite because he was fast and fun. I chose Phil so I could put myself in a forward flanking position to guarantee we made the first left turn and outrun the horses if I needed to. The other girls were assigned reliable jingle horses and were instructed to either flank the herd or push the herd. The cowboys filtered in on their own horses, positioning themselves next to the girl they seemed the most interested in hitting on later that night.

As we exited the corral out the back gate, we prepared to make a sharp left turn to get the horses headed toward the back road, where we would need to turn right—and from there, it was going to be a straight shot to the back pasture. With two lead horses, several flankers, and more than enough pushers, the excitement between humans and animals was palpable. The horses came out hot, but that was no surprise; after being cooped up for so long in a strange corral, they were more than ready to move.

We navigated the first left turn effortlessly as the horses eagerly followed Wilma and Gypsy. The girls were flanking the horses perfectly, and I giggled as I watched the cowboys quickly realize that they should have been paying attention when we went over the plan. Their horses weren't accustomed to a herd of one hundred horses running at them. I watched, bemused, as their horses reared and shied, rendering them helpless. *Poor Beau,* I thought sarcastically. *You had no idea what your boys were walking into.*

As we approached the right turn, the horses moved in tandem, and the girls were still doing their job flawlessly. If we managed to make this right turn, the straight line to the pasture would be in clear sight.

Unfortunately, the horses had another plan in mind. The flankers on the left of the herd started yelling at the tops of their lungs and waving their flags, trying to turn the herd, as Lady decided she had no interest in following Wilma and Gypsy that day. She blew past the flankers as if they weren't even there, and the rest of the herd followed, going straight up a narrow road that led toward the steep ledge of a small mountain in the complete opposite direction of the pasture we were trying to get to. At this point, I had no idea where they were headed, and I'm sure they didn't either.

I yelled to everyone. "Hold up! Don't chase them!"

I watched in shock as the scene unfolded before my eyes. Instead of heading toward the pasture, the horses continued to run up the small mountain, fanning out like a scene from *The Man from Snowy River*, where all the horses galloped at full speed like a herd of wild mustangs.

Damn you, Lady! As I cursed her, part of me watched in awe as Lady, notorious for taking the herd wherever she wanted, led the group astray. Lady had long been retired and hadn't done this in years, but there she was, reliving her youth and running as fast as she could with the rest of the herd following.

I pulled on Phil's reins. "Whoa!"

The one thing I had learned in my time wrangling was that there was no reason to keep chasing the horses; they would stop . . . eventually. I yelled to the girls to stop as well, but despite my admonition, the cowboys and Lexi decided to keep chasing them, hooting and hollering at the tops of their lungs.

Suddenly, the easy mile jingle was out of control. *Are they still on ranch property?* I attempted to envision a mental map of the area but felt disoriented the farther the horses got from the pasture. By this point, the horses were long gone, and I could only hope they had decided to stop on their own.

I called the girls around me. "Ladies, it's time for Plan B." I thought frantically and decided the solution was to spread out and slowly start searching for them. I asked Allison to call Lexi to see if she had come to her senses and had managed to stop the boys from chasing the horses any farther.

Next, I directed the group to make their way up the steep hill and then spread out; from there, we would locate the herd, gather them up again, then try and take them back to the corral where we'd started. If we managed to do that, we could attempt this crazy plan all over again. But this time, I would make sure I put myself on the left side, with a wall of flankers.

But first, we had to figure out where those damn horses went.

Meanwhile, the girls were having a blast with the unexpected turn of events; Jessica and Kyra somehow managed to flirt with the Smith boys as they galloped past, winking and trash-talking in a way that was sure to attract the admiration of the cowboys, who would be impressed with the girls' wrangling skills. Deep down, a small part of me was enjoying this chaotic scene as much as they were, but as their leader, I needed to literally rein in my own adventurous spirit and get everyone back into formation.

As we walked up the steep hill and began to spread out, I couldn't help but think about how far I had come. I was no longer in a suit and heels, and the days of my wannabe show jumping career were long gone. In this moment, the girls were all working as a team, and I was at the helm, directing them like I had done this all my life. There was no time for insecurities or self-doubt—and personally, I couldn't be prouder of the girls and their abilities. Who said hunter/jumper girls couldn't wrangle?

Thankfully, the horses came into view, scattered among the trees. They were everywhere. We would need to gather them up slowly and then start this crazy ride all over again, back to where we'd come from.

I calculated how dangerous navigating the hairpin turn would be, deciding it was just too dangerous, no matter how tempting it was to do whatever it took in the moment to regain a sense of organization. We would need to head back to the corrals, as it wasn't worth risking any of the horses or wranglers getting hurt.

I somehow managed to pull out my cell phone and dial Joey's number. I needed to make sure he and the other ranch hands were working on getting us hay and equipment. He no sooner picked up than I breathlessly explained what was happening, just as Phil decided to throw a giant buck in playful anticipation of what he seemed to think would be the next yeehaw ride.

"Joey, we lost the herd—but we got them back!" I yelled. "Were you able to get hay out? Any updates on the fire? And, of course, Phil here is having a blast, bucking and playing, but I've got to get this group back together, Joey!"

I jumped from topic to topic, unaware that I sounded a bit crazed at the moment, not giving Joey a chance to get a word in edgewise.

He laughed, somehow following my scattered statements.

"Sounds like Phil! Listen, you've got this, Emme. You're a long way from your lawyer days, but you'll figure it all out. You usually do. Try to enjoy this memorable moment! I know that sounds strange, but I can tell this is the adventure of a lifetime, and anyone who lives on a ranch has a little bit of that daredevil nature to 'em! Plus, I know you'll still manage to keep everyone safe. To be honest, I'm jealous I'm not there riding with you. You always make the right decisions for the horses. I've already taken a few loads of hay over, and I'll make sure you have everything you need once you get the horses into the pasture!"

After I ended the call, I smiled and shoved the phone into my back pocket. *Joey's right. I need to appreciate the moment, even if I feel a bit terrified too. Things didn't go according to plan, but I've got the best wranglers around, and we're going to get these horses where they need to go, despite our little detour. And thank God for Joey. I can always rely on him to take care of things.*

I took in the scene. Clouds of dust and dirt filled the air, and a few horses were losing their footing but righting themselves without any apparent injury. Girls were hooting and hollering, and the boys were busy whistling and catcalling after them. The chaos couldn't have been better choreographed. It looked like a scene from a Wild West movie!

After giving everyone a few minutes to play and enjoy the moment, I whistled and got their attention to regroup and refocus on their original mission: following Phil and me back to the main corral, with the horses' safety as our number-one priority. The wranglers reluctantly steered their horses in my direction, and within a few short minutes, everyone was back on track, headed to the Smith ranch, albeit on a detour.

While the wranglers loved the horses as much as I did, I felt it was my responsibility to redirect them when the excitement of a great ride distracted them from the very real dangers we were facing. *How very Russell-like of me!* I also wanted to make sure they didn't lose sight of the gravity of the situation. As much as they wanted to pretend the fire wasn't that bad and that everything was under control, my earlier optimism was giving way to worry once more.

We gathered the horses and took off again, back to the ranch, galloping downhill on the side of a cliff among a hundred crazed horses. This was not something I'd ever envisioned myself doing, but my team was having a blast, feeling the rush of adrenaline that only comes from simultaneously doing something exciting and slightly dangerous.

Once we got them in the corral, we needed to make this ride all over again. Except this time, we would make that dang right turn! Learning from my mistakes, I also vowed that we would have a goddamn wall of wranglers flanking the herd on the left side to guarantee everything would go smoothly and we would make the right turn toward the pasture.

This time, within twenty minutes, our second attempt was complete. The boys finally understood their job, and they had successfully assisted the girls and me in forming a wall. The horses made the right turn perfectly as they followed Wilma and Gypsy down the mile-long road to their new home.

Once we arrived at the pasture, the horses scattered again, bucking and playing while they explored their new temporary home.

I checked my watch as we trotted back to the gate, glad it was only one thirty in the afternoon. *Plenty of time to acclimate everyone before nightfall.* The horses appeared happy with their new digs as they explored the property and nudged their equine friends approvingly.

I looked at the wranglers, and they looked at me with dirt smeared on their faces and covering their teeth, grinning ear to ear.

"Okay, gang," I stated. "Time for a quick lunch break. And then we need to get the next hundred horses here."

Kyra joked, "Woo-hoo, Emme. Same route again, right?"

I smiled wryly. "Yeah, Kyra. Let's *not* do that again, okay?" I paused and then added, "I know, that was absolutely insane. But let's not tempt fate, guys! Let me think on the plan for this group, since the other horses are across the road, a mile or so away."

Everyone groaned as if they thought I might have been planning the same wild ride a second time. Kyra hopped off her horse and started playing music on her phone as the girls and guys began dancing around in celebration of their first success of the day.

She yelled over to me, "We get it, Emme! We'd never put the horses in harm's way. And you know we're going to do whatever you tell us to do. We trust that your plan is going to keep all of us safe too. But let's take a minute to enjoy that insane jingle because we all killed it! You've got the best damn wranglers right here, so don't let anyone forget that!"

Kyra pranced around and shimmied her hips, successfully attracting glances from more than one cowboy. Then, like a desert mirage, Joey showed up with sandwiches and beers. I grinned. We would take a much-needed break—and then we would start moving the other horses.

I smiled at everyone's naivete but allowed them to have their fun for a few moments. As they basked in the afterglow of the crazy yet successful jingle, I plopped down on the ground and started planning how we would move the remaining horses.

There must be an easier way to do this.

OCTOBER 17, 2020
2:30 PM

It was time to move the next group, and I finally had made up my mind: considering the previous jingle, I needed to plan a safer option. Besides, everyone was exhausted from the eighteen-hour day yesterday and the nonstop action from this morning. Not only that, but I wanted to be home before midnight. At the same time, I was starting to wonder what the fire was doing.

In preparation for my announcement, I called the girls, Smith cowboys, ranch owners, and other volunteers who had made their way to the Smith ranch after hearing about the first jingle, hoping for some fun of their own.

"Although safety is my top priority, I will admit that the insanity of that jingle also made it one of the best rides of my entire life." I paused, allowing the wranglers a moment to cheer in agreement. "However, it's time for a reality check, and I need to take everyone's safety into account. It's not an exaggeration to say we got lucky. Between the fence line and metal scraps, it's a minor miracle that no one went through the barbed wire, stepped on metal, or even just stepped into a hole and broke their leg. Not to mention the fact that the route from the Brightside ranch to the Smiths' is not nearly as clear-cut as the last path."

I allowed my words to sink in to prepare everyone for what I was about to say. "So, with that being said, I decided that we're not doing another jingle. We are going to ride and pony the next hundred horses over to the Smith ranch from the Brightside ranch. It should take us a couple of hours to get all the horses over there. Then we will drop hay since there isn't much grass in the pasture."

To "pony" the horses meant using halters and ropes to attach the horses without riders to the horses we were riding. Although there were inherent risks to this approach, in my opinion, it was the safer option.

I did my best to ignore the collective groaning and eye-rolling before continuing, but it wasn't easy, especially when I heard Allison grumble under her breath, "Buzzkill!"

"I know, I know. It'll take hours and not minutes. But it's the safest decision. And for that reason, it's my final decision."

I forced myself to hold my head high to appear confident, although I was struggling to make eye contact with anyone, knowing they were disappointed in the decision. They all wanted another wild jingle!

At that moment, the normally quiet Molly piped up. "Emme, I get it. You're making the best decision for the horses. It's the right thing to do. Besides, I'm exhausted, and I am sure everyone else is as well."

A few of the girls nodded reluctantly as they loaded their tack and equipment into the truck. I silently thanked Molly, making a mental note to thank her privately later for the support.

We all climbed in the truck and drove the two miles over to the Brightside ranch, where the rest of the herd was being pastured.

When we arrived at the Brightsides' place, I instructed the girls to each pick a group of horses and ride the easiest one. This time, I rode Fred. (Any excuse to ride my favorite guest horse!) Josie, Britches, and Paint Jack followed to my right. On my left, two old kids' horses, Hombre and Muchacho, followed along, tied to my saddle horn and more than willing to follow their friend, Fred. Thankfully, Fred responded well to me since I was too busy concentrating on not dropping the other three horses' ropes to pay much attention to my own trusty horse.

Ponying one hundred horses over a mile, several times, felt painstakingly slow after the previous joyride, but with the help of the wranglers and additional volunteers (including Dr. Hecksher, her six-horse trailer, and one man with a two-horse trailer), we were able to move the group slowly but safely to their destination.

The second arrival at the Smith ranch was met with significantly less fanfare, and I breathed a sigh of relief.

We made it. A hundred and ninety-two horses, safely together in their temporary home . . . and it's only seven thirty!

Everyone else must have realized the night was still young, as Joey shouted, "Where do we go tonight, ladies?"

My wranglers yelled out names of various local bars, and I watched these girls—far younger than me—climb into the Smith cowboys' trucks and head to that evening's watering hole.

Despite feeling celebratory myself, I honestly wanted nothing more than to go home to Tom and climb into bed.

OCTOBER 17, 2020
9:00 PM

Tom stood close to the television, listening intently to the fire chief's updates during the latest broadcast. I, on the other hand, couldn't move off the couch. I was way too exhausted after the day's excitement to even pay attention to the chief's words. Closing my eyes, I smiled, relieved that all the horses were finally reunited and pastured together in the same place that night.

My last thought before drifting off was that I should probably ask Tom if there was any new information. I was hopeful that the update had been the same as before—no risk of the fire reaching the ranch.

"Honey?" I could hear Tom's voice, but it was barely registering.

"Hmm?"

"Never mind. It can wait until morning . . ."

I nodded and promptly fell into a much-needed slumber.

C LAZY U: GETTING PROMOTED

Russell shook my hand, but I was in shock. *I got the promotion?*

He turned to the other girls in the room after making the announcement that I would be the new head wrangler. The time had passed quickly, and my six-month trial at the ranch had turned into two years. And although I loved what I did every day, there was still a little voice in the back of my mind that reminded me that, despite the raise, I would eventually need to return to law. How else could I pay off all those student loans?

The year before, I'd interviewed with several firms in Colorado. Thankfully, my half-hearted attempts had flopped. The interviewers could clearly see my heart was still with riding—not the law. But those interview fails had positioned me for this moment: as head wrangler.

What's a few more years on the ranch? I can go back to law later.

Despite Russell's endorsement, I knew that Allison, Kyra, and the rest of the wrangling crew had hoped Russell would promote Andrew, the foreman. But what they didn't know (because Russell had confided this to me only minutes earlier) was that Andrew had lost his temper with the horses one too many times for Russell's liking and was hitting the bottle way too hard as of late.

"Emme," Russell had drawled as the two of us stood in his office before the formal announcement. "I know you may never completely lose that let's-get-it-done Northeast attitude. But you manage to set that aside when you're with the horses. There's a calmness about you that they respect and follow." He chuckled and lowered his voice. "Plus, you can ride anything you can swing your leg over better than Andrew any day—even if your stirrups are a hole shorter than they should be and you still ride with that silly arch in your back!"

I laughed. He was right: all those years of English lessons and equitation classes didn't disappear just because the tack changed.

Although Russell's words warmed my heart, I knew the girls were going to take the news differently, and I was right about that. As soon as the words were out of his mouth, I heard Allison whisper snidely to Kyra, "Anyone in this room would have been more qualified than *her*."

I fought back my urge to scream and reminded myself that they didn't know what Russell had shared about Andrew. Hell, they still didn't believe that a lawyer might want to leave it all behind to live on a dude ranch. Even after all this time, they acted as if this was all some hoax— as if I was going to surprise them with a camera crew from *Punk'd* and say, "You're right, everyone! This was all one big sham."

I also knew that due to their youth, they weren't considering the importance of maturity in this type of position. I had at least ten to fifteen years on most of the girls. And even though they had been on equine career paths right out of the gate, I'd had time on my side—time to visit the ranch as a guest and years of riding and showing with some of the best trainers around—along with my business savvy from my former day job. In a way, that became an asset in Russell's eyes.

Allison's shrill voice cut through the silence. "Guess what, everyone? I just got a text from Andrew. He's quitting, effective tomorrow. But I guess you two don't care, huh?" Allison pointed at Russell and me.

I rolled my eyes, shocked at her audacity. *She's totally out of line!*

I had heard the rumors circulating that Allison was involved with Andrew—or, at the very least, *wanted* to be. But I knew this was one of her attention-seeking tactics designed to both make it look like she was in the know about ranch happenings and knock Russell and me down a peg. However, I knew if I tried to defend Russell, I was going to be fighting even more of an uphill battle than I already had before me.

Thankfully, Russell came to the rescue.

"Allison, with all due respect, I need you to take a breath and back up. You're out of line." He glared at her in a way I had never seen him look at anyone, and Allison actually lowered her head shamefully. But Russell wasn't finished.

"Now, listen here. Y'all may think you know what's best for this ranch, considering you are in your *first and second* years of wrangling. But have I ever led any of you astray?" Silence. "That's a question, ladies."

"No, Russell," they mumbled as if they were being reprimanded by their father.

Russell nodded. "That's what I thought. So, what makes you think this decision is something that might not be in the best interests of the ranch, the horses, or everyone in this room?" This time, he allowed the rhetorical question to hang in the air.

They all knew he was right. Russell's decision-making was the best, bar none. And for them to question him was an exercise in folly.

"Emme's no different than me, ladies. She puts the horses ahead of everyone—ahead of herself, for Chrissake—so it's time you get off your own high horses and pay her some respect."

The girls hung their heads, silently acknowledging that Russell was right—as usual.

As the girls filed out of the room, Russell motioned for me to follow him back to his office. I stepped inside, and he closed the door. Tears of happiness and sadness streamed down my face.

Russell handed me a box of tissues. "Hey, kid. I know that was tough. And unfortunately, I knew they would react like that." I sniffed and blotted my eyes with the Kleenex. "Don't take it personally. They would have had that same reaction with anyone taking over for me. No one likes change, Emme. I meant it when I said I made the right decision. But now it's time for *you* to believe that for yourself." Russell's eyes bore into mine. "So here's my final farewell advice, which will work wonders with the girls: treat them like the horses, and don't push too much. Just like the horses want to feel like they have some control, get a sense of when to apply pressure and how much. You've got spot-on instincts with all the horses here; just apply those instincts to the girls, and you'll be golden."

I considered Russell's words and, for the millionth time, admitted he was right. "Thanks, Russell," I said as he gave me a big bear hug.

Then he straightened himself and coughed.

Is that a tear in his eye? But before I could know for sure, he patted me on the back and pushed the phone on his desk toward me.

"Now, enough of this crying stuff," he said. "Time to celebrate! Call that husband of yours. Hell, call your parents too. C Lazy U can handle the long-distance bill." He chuckled. "Congratulations, Emme."

* * *

"Mom? Guess what?"

The minute I'd hung up with Tom, I'd dialed my parents' number. I could imagine my mom sitting at the island in the kitchen, twisting around her fingers the old phone cord that she refused to upgrade.

"What, honey?"

"You're talking to the official head wrangler at C Lazy U Ranch!"

She paused. "Honey, that's fantastic! Not exactly the reason I thought you were calling, but congratulations! You're going to make an amazing lead wrangler."

"*Head* wrangler, Mom." I smiled, tears welling up again in my eyes. Mom tried to cover, but her slipup of "Not exactly the reason I thought you were calling" reminded me of the many conversations we'd had about why Tom and I didn't have kids yet. Despite the fact that we were newly married, Mom wanted nothing more than to have grandkids. And while the people pleaser in me vacillated at times in wanting to give her that gift, I knew in my soul that the ranch and horses were my heart—and that it wouldn't be fair to a child if I couldn't devote my all to a family.

Fortunately, Tom understood and supported my decision to give up my law career and stay on to work at the ranch. In fact, he frequently mentioned how proud of me he was for not following the money by moving to the city and returning to law. However, that decision meant that every couple of months, I needed to remind my mother of these things. I knew we would have kids one day, but I wanted to work my new job for a year or two first.

Recently, she had stopped the light badgering, so I wasn't too upset with her unintentional comment. Instead, I forced myself to focus on her affirmation: *You're going to make an amazing head wrangler.*

She coughed and then added, "You know, Emme, it's never too late to go back to law either. You've only been gone a couple of years, and you could easily find a firm in Denver." She paused, and when I didn't speak, I could tell she knew that was not going to happen anytime soon. "Well, I know you've had this sweet cowgirl fantasy for so long, but just in case you ever need a backup plan . . ."

"Thanks, Mom, but we're fine. Really."

After I hung up the phone, I exhaled and grinned. *Damn the haters. I'm going to prove to them that I was the right choice. And I'm going to win those girls over in the process! I'll make Russell proud—and myself too.*

CHAPTER 7

LOSING CONTROL

OCTOBER 21, 2020

8:00 AM

As I drove past C Lazy U, headed toward the Smith ranch, where the horses were currently safe, I marveled at the stark contrast between the wild chaos of the jingles from a few days before and this almost eerily calm operation to ready the ranch.

Ready the ranch.

I rolled the phrase around in my head, wondering what would happen if we really needed to be ready for anything else. Truth be told, I was exhausted thinking of the what-ifs and wanted to take a few minutes to bask in the calm. For once, I wanted to be glass-half-full Emme: a girl who expected the best in every situation.

I should be optimistic! I told myself. *The weather is cooperating, and it's just a matter of time before everyone can return to the ranch and return to normal. After all, it has been almost a week, and the fire seems to be under control.*

The firefighters and insurance company representatives roamed the ranch property, knocking on doors of the multimillion-dollar ranch homes and reassuring residents that their property would be covered if any worst-case scenario occurred. Other firefighters conducted controlled burns of the deadfall while Tom and his guys helped cut back trees near the homes and ranch buildings. Meanwhile, the remaining ranch staff methodically removed artifacts from the cabins and deep-cleaned the rooms.

I parked and walked up the steps to Hattie's kitchen for a quick cup of coffee; I felt a strong need for caffeine and conversation before taking care of the horses in the back pasture. But before I could knock on the door, my phone lit up. I smiled at the text from Molly that assured me that the thirty-five tons of hay they'd removed earlier from the ranch had just arrived at the evacuation pasture, as we were referring to it. *Molly's really showing her leadership.* Not only had she become the de facto liaison between the girls and me, but she tirelessly provided information to the staff each night, from giving fire updates to filling everyone in on what each team accomplished and reassuring anyone who texted to ask if the town of Grand Lake was in danger. ("It's not!" Molly would reply.) Although this crazy fire had spread across almost thirty thousand acres, it finally seemed to be under control.

I knocked, and as soon as Hattie opened the weathered wooden door, she put her hand on my shoulder, and we walked toward the kitchen in silence.

"Hey there, Emme. Whatcha thinkin' about?"

The Smith ranch had been in Hattie's family since the late 1800s, so if anyone should be nervous about losing it all, it would be Hattie. And even though we'd both immediately hit it off when we met a few years back due to our shared Philadelphia roots—Hattie had spent time studying at Penn before moving out West too—she hadn't inherited that fast-paced anxiety that is so prevalent among those hailing from the City of Brotherly Love.

I turned to Hattie and smiled. "Just thinking about how calm everything is right now. And wondering how long it'll stay that way." I giggled, knowing Hattie would give me a hard time for my waiting-for-the-other-shoe-to-drop mentality.

Hattie didn't disappoint. "Emme, at what point are you going to get on board with the rest of the Coloradans and stop your needless worry . . . at least, until you *really* have something to worry about?" She laughed. "Then again, I guess you lawyers don't get where you are in life by assuming the best."

I sighed. "You're right, Hattie. I probably wouldn't have made it too far if I believed every story clients and opposing counsel told me. But I sometimes wish I could turn off my cynical brain when it comes to this fire. But seriously, this fire is far from trivial. I mean, how is it that you don't panic? This is your home. Your land!"

Hattie smiled, exuding a sense of peace and calm—mixed with typical Hattie humor—that only comes with age. "Of course, this land feels like a part of me, but if the Lord decides it's time for it to go, that's His decision." She leaned in close and whispered, "To be honest, I have been panicking just a little. But fortunately, I got good news! My psychic told me that everything is working out for my highest good. And then my pastor talked about God's bounty last Sunday, so I said to myself, 'Hell, if those two are telling me everything is going to be okay, who am I to doubt them?' They're way more connected with something bigger than me, so I've just gotta trust."

I grinned. *Who would've thought that a pastor and a psychic would be on the same wavelength? And apparently, Hattie has taken a huge dose of denial!*

Hattie scoffed. "Plus, you can't beat Mother Nature. That's just a fact. And in my mind, as long as it's not some fella in a suit and starched shirt taking the land from me, I'm at peace."

Now it was my turn to laugh. Hattie had made it known how much she hated lawyers—one in particular, thanks to some never-to-be-forgotten lawsuit in which a greedy developer tried to serve Hattie's family. Apparently, this lawyer, who happened to be the heir of an oil magnate, decided he wanted to spend his daddy's money by taking over the Smith ranch and turning it into a condo community. I remembered the day she told me about his attempt to convince a judge that the land didn't belong to Hattie's family due to some outdated legal code that claimed two square feet of the property was considered multi-living space and thereby all thirty-five thousand acres should be handed over to him.

"That greedy bastard would have needed to take me to court in handcuffs before I would have let him turn this place into some goddamn fifty-five-plus community, with basket weaving and Bingo. But if that fancy lawyer with his fancy words thought he was going to outsmart my family . . . Well, they didn't know we had some *cowboy* legal aid, if you know what I mean!"

Off the record, Hattie had shared the details of how the case died: some family friends who happened to have a little bit of legal training—and a lot of bourbon—went rogue one evening and paid the lawyer a visit at his hotel. "Nothin' physical, mind you. We're not the mob!" Hattie had said, laughing. "I think they just used their colorful language and art of persuasion—which some may call a 'threat'—and got him to drop his ridiculous suit."

So, knowing how much she distrusted lawyers, I was happy when we first met and Hattie said she'd give me a chance before writing me off as another greedy bastard. I must've passed the test, because now, whenever Hattie and I talked, it was about the Eagles, the Phillies, Wawa, or who had the best cheesesteaks—Pat's or Gino's. But today, it was all about her family's ranch and my love for the C Lazy U.

Hattie continued. "Emme, I appreciate your concern. It means you really understand how much this ranch means to my family. So let's just say our prayers and leave it up to the big guy upstairs." She turned to walk away but stopped and turned back to face me. "Oh yeah, I almost forgot! If this crazy fire storm changes direction and you and Tom need to evacuate at some point, you're more than welcome to stay here this winter. Well, actually, stay as long as you need. The same goes for all the C Lazy U horses. If C Lazy U burns and you are not able to go home, we will figure out how to make it work. So, don't worry."

"Thanks, Hattie! Hopefully, it doesn't come to that. I've already skipped too many doctor appointments."

Hattie raised her eyebrows and whispered, "IVF?"

I nodded. Hattie was one of the few people who knew I'd finally caved and had taken out another loan for a second round. To be honest, I tried not to think about it, considering how expensive it was and how much of a reach it was for Tom and me financially. I was also trying not to focus too much on the first IVF treatment not taking. I had already shed so many tears when we got the bad news. But truth be told, I wasn't the best patient either, what with work taking every moment of my day and forcing me to cancel more appointments than I would like to admit. And while Tom sometimes got frustrated when I told him I had to cancel yet another appointment, he understood; he, too, was married to work at times. And right now, the fire and saving the C Lazy U and the horses had to remain our top priority. The horses were pretty much my children anyway.

But wouldn't Mom be over the moon if I called her to tell her the IVF took? She would be shocked, since I wasn't going to tell her about the IVF unless I got pregnant. *No use getting anyone's hopes up.*

OCTOBER 21, 2020
2:00 PM

As I fed the horses, I looked up at the sky. *Was that mushroom cloud over there before?* I squinted to get a better view, considering part of the county was smothered in a blanket of thick smoke.

Trying to shake off the worry, I walked to the feed wagon. As I got up on the step to lift myself up, a wind gust passed through and almost blew me off the wagon. I braced myself as if I were grounding my legs like a tree forming roots. The winds were kicking up again, and some of the gusts had to be blowing at sixty miles an hour, minimum. I pulled my phone out of my pocket and looked with horror at the weather app's warning: red flag. *Again.*

I fed the horses quickly, checking on everyone as best I could and taking a couple of extra minutes to spend some quality time with Trigger and Fred. Then I drove back to the ranch in a panic. However, the scene before me when I arrived was one of tranquility: firefighters were reassuring everyone that their structure protection teams would take care of everything, and the ranch staff were taking a break, sitting around talking.

I shook my head and pushed the worrying thoughts to the back of my mind. *We're out of the danger zone. That red-flag day warning is just that: a precaution.*

OCTOBER 21, 2020
4:30 PM

As Tom maneuvered the truck toward the ranch gates, I saw the red glow of police lights in the rearview mirror. The law enforcement caravan following us and our vehicle packed with last-minute items from the office gave me a feeling of safety, as if the fire couldn't touch us if the police were there, protecting us.

It's silly to think that the men in blue could ward off a natural disaster, but this irrational thought is better than having a panic attack!

Tom mused, "Other than that dark smoke and red glow, this doesn't seem much different from the day we got the pre-evacuation order." I nodded in agreement as the truck approached the crest of the hill, where we drove through the exit gates.

Before I could say anything, I noticed Tom gripping the wheel. I followed his gaze and looked straight ahead, where large flames seemingly appeared out of nowhere, dancing across McQueary's Ridge, which was situated directly across the street from the ranch and about a quarter of a mile away. And as if Mother Nature wanted to set the mood for terror, wind gusts of ninety miles an hour shook our truck, so much so that Tom struggled to maintain a straight line.

I might be crazy, but it feels like the fire is actually creating its own weather conditions! What the hell?

Within seconds, the sky turned black as the smoke obscured the sun. If I didn't know what time it was, I would have thought we were driving through the middle of the night.

My phone lit up again. It was Jack.

"Hello?" I said.

"Emme, I really need your help. Grand Lake is now under mandatory evacuation orders." Jack's voice trailed off, and I could hear the deep breaths he was taking, apparently to calm himself down. *He sounds absolutely terrified! This is 100 percent not like him.*

I gripped the phone tightly as he continued. "Please see if you and Tom can pick up Wendy and the kids. I can't believe I didn't realize until now that they might be in danger! What the hell was I thinking?" He started breathing heavily again, and now it was my turn to calm someone down.

"Jack, it's okay. Tom and I are really close to your place, so please don't worry! And don't beat yourself up either. We've all been so focused on the ranch that it was easier to assume everyone else was okay! I am sure your family is fine, and we'll get there as quickly as we can! Hang in there."

As the truck made the left turn onto US-34 and rambled down the road toward Grand Lake, I stared, saucer-eyed, at the scene playing before me as if I were in the middle of a Hollywood movie set: flames that looked like firebombs or meteors exploding, as if we were in a war zone . . . a field in the distance, consumed with flames . . . wildlife running frantically . . . trees lying across the road, upended by the intense wind gusts.

Oh. My. God.

Tom hit the accelerator, yet it appeared that the hillside was exploding faster than we could drive. After several minutes, he pulled off to the side of the road. I was numb with disbelief as we wordlessly got out of the truck and stared at the awesome sight. For some reason, the fear I felt moments earlier froze in time as Tom and I stared with awe and wonder at Mother Nature's light show, as if she were reminding us how small we really were in the grand scheme of things.

"What the fuck is that?" I screamed. The blaze was now burning with such intensity that a black, fluffy creation pressed down to the ground and bottomed out in dark, inklike patterns. I later learned that experts call this a pyrocumulus cloud, and it had formed a column collapse, where the plume above the fire fell under its own weight. Meanwhile, the cool air supercharged the flames with a rush of fresh oxygen. But in that moment, it simply looked like a canvas with dark paint smeared over it in asymmetrical patterns that kept shifting and changing.

My phone rang, and I swiped across the screen to answer it. "Hello?"

"Emme, this is Officer Pete. I was in the car behind you and noticed you and Tom pulled over. I wanted to let you know I just got word that the fire's pace has accelerated to six thousand acres per hour. You don't need to panic, but conditions are deteriorating, quickly. Wind gusts up to a hundred miles per hour and downed power lines. I know what we're witnessing is an unbelievable sight, but I think you and Tom would be best served getting back into your car and driving to safety."

My fear returned. In shock, I nodded and raced back to the passenger door. I hung up without even saying goodbye and dug my fingernails into my palms, hoping to stay calm before speaking. My fear had returned in full force.

"Tom, it's getting worse. We need to go to staff housing in town and check on everyone."

Tom, who knew better than to ask questions, simply nodded, gripped the wheel even harder, and made a U-turn toward town. We just had to hope and pray that Jack's wife, Wendy, and their children were safely evacuating.

Fortunately, we were only a few miles from the old motel where the majority of the staff were bunked up. As we walked through the door of the building, I exhaled with relief, realizing that the overly crowded room was a good sign that everyone had made it to safety.

But never one to assume, I took another deep breath and motioned for attention. When the room grew silent, I said, "Hey, it looks like we're all here, but just to be sure, I think we need a buddy system."

Lexi and Molly methodically reviewed the staff list, and they assigned each staff member a partner. That person would be responsible for either making sure their buddy was in the room or calling them to ensure they were somewhere safe. Everyone began waving toward their partners, and those who couldn't find their buddy started texting and calling. Meanwhile, Tom worked with Jack and some of the ranch hands to make sure we could feed everyone. We had been so busy worrying about the ranch that it was time to make sure our team was nourished!

Knowing that our staff—most of them just out of college—needed consolation and reassurance allowed me to push my own fears to the side and walk around, hugging some of the girls and guys who were obviously traumatized and giving pats on the back to the ones who were keeping a stiff upper lip (but were probably breaking down inside). No one could believe the ranch might be burning—or that the residents of Grand Lake were being evacuated without any notice because of how quickly the fire was moving.

After circulating around the room, I stepped into a small alcove adjacent to the large room, where Tom had set up a makeshift office, equipped with a tiny table, folding chair, and his laptop. He was clicking away, zooming in and out of the maps that showed the fire's predicted trajectory. I could see that the path—ever since the winds had shifted again—was taking it toward Rocky Mountain National Park, on the west side of Grand Lake and nowhere near the horses. I pulled my cell phone from my pocket and dialed Hattie's number.

"Hi, Emme! What's up?"

"Not much. Just checking to see how the horses are doing and if you have heard whether you will be going under a pre-evacuation order."

Hattie chuckled. "Em, nothing has happened since you left earlier today. Everyone is fine: Horses. Pasture. Me!"

I could picture Hattie sitting in her kitchen, winding around her finger the cord of the old-fashioned phone she refused to get rid of.

She added, "I have heard that Grand Lake is now under a mandatory evacuation order. Sounds like some residents are stuck and can't get out. But thank the good Lord that everyone still says the fire will skip Granby, so it seems like we're okay for the night at the very least! I know anything can happen, but we are okay for the time being. And so are the horses."

I sighed. "Okay. Thanks, Hattie! Glad everyone— including you!—is doing well. Take care. Call me tomorrow, and we will reevaluate."

I put my phone back into my pocket as Molly approached Tom and me. She had just gotten off the phone with her assigned buddy.

"Well, Kai's fine," she said. "Thank God! She's frantically loading all her belongings in her car, just in case the wind shifts again and Granby goes under an evacuation order. You know, most staff who aren't here are probably doing the same thing. Packing up their stuff."

My mind flashed to the people in Grand Lake who'd just lost everything because they weren't afforded any time to pack up.

Shit. Tom and I should probably do the same.

OCTOBER 21, 2020
2:00 AM

I lay in bed, eyes wide open, listening to the emergency radio dispatch. Based on his breathing, I could tell that even Tom, a typically heavy sleeper, was still awake. Neither one of us was going to get much sleep. All we could do was lie there and worry and listen to the radio frequency through an app Tom had discovered on his phone.

Then the thought hit me, and I bolted upright in the bed.

"Tom? Did you pack the coffee maker?"

He rolled toward me and laughed. "Yes, Emme, we packed it. When I said to pack the most important things, I didn't realize the Keurig fit into that category!"

I smiled for the first time in hours. "You're right. I guess my cup of joe isn't life or death. But when you think about it, what do I really have that's all that important? Not much. Just a pair of jeans, my favorite shirt, my English saddle, wedding rings, family albums, and some files." I giggled, almost delirious from lack of sleep. "I think there was room for some coffee! I mean, if we make it out alive, aren't we going to need caffeine to keep us going after all of this sleep deprivation?"

"Good point, Emme. I can't believe our home may be in danger, but better safe than sorry. Plus—"

The dispatcher's voice crackled over the radio, and now Tom sat up to listen to her staccato sentence fragments.

"Fire expanding to 125,678 acres . . . A couple miles from town of Granby, parts of Grand Lake still burning, Rocky Mountain National Park burning . . . Hundreds of structures burning . . . Grand Lake Lodge intact . . . No known injuries or fatalities at this time . . . Miller ranch intact . . . C Lazy U Ranch intact . . . More updates to come shortly."

Despite the fact that this news meant we might need to evacuate at any second, all I heard was "C Lazy U Ranch intact." I jumped out of bed and ran around to Tom's side. I wrapped my arms around his shoulders and squeezed with great excitement.

"Did you hear that? C Lazy U has been spared!"

He squeezed me back. "Thank God! The ranch made it!"

Crying with relief, I proclaimed, "Everything is going to be okay! It just has to be!"

BCLU
OCTOBER 1995

"I'll give a hundred bucks to anyone who drinks with me before Crozer's chem lab tomorrow."

Drew Laniere looked around the bonfire, challenging one of us to agree to his dare. Most of the guys looked down, and the ones who didn't just laughed at Drew's really bad idea.

That particular night, it was just Laura and me hanging out with the group, but I didn't mind. Truth be told, I felt more comfortable around the guys at my high school than the petty girls who pretended to be my friends. They were more concerned about the label on your jeans or your bag, or your ability to help them advance their social status, than whether you were interesting, smart, or had a personality. Since I had no boyfriend and no guy actually interested in me, I really didn't matter much to them anyway. And none of them cared about horses—except for Laura.

I looked at my friend to see her reaction to Drew's comment, but she was already falling asleep after one too many Yuengling lagers. Mentally, I imagined myself in my parents' basement, where they had a fully stocked bar, ready for impromptu get-togethers with the neighbors. I knew there were multiple bottles of vodka behind the bar since some of the ladies' new obsession was Sex on the Beach.

Feeling emboldened from the couple of drinks I had downed in Laura's bedroom before meeting up with the group in the woods—and trying to get Drew to notice me—I raised my hand. "I'll do it!" I laughed. "I could use a hundred bucks!"

Drew fist-pumped the air and high-fived me. "Look who's got the balls in this group! Okay, Emme, let's see what you're made of. Tomorrow, fifth period. Meet me outside the boys' locker room. No one has gym at that time. And guess who's got keys to the locker room!"

Drew smiled, and everyone groaned. Ever since he'd become captain of the football team (a losing team, I might add), Drew had to make sure everyone knew all the perks he'd received with this accomplishment.

I was on top of the world, giddy with relief that Drew, of all people, was paying attention to me. Getting someone to express romantic interest had become a recent obsession, considering I was the only virgin in my friend group. Making matters worse, everyone at the barn kept reminding me that if I was ever going to hook up with some older guy in the horse world who could lavish gifts and money on me, I'd better get some practice so I could be confident I was good in bed for someone more experienced.

I took a puff on the cigarette someone handed me, I guess as a gift for being the only one stupid enough to go along with Drew's misguided idea. Resisting the urge to cough (*How does anyone enjoy smoking?*), I mustered a smile that I hoped looked like confidence.

Everyone else seems to be fitting in without any problems. So what's wrong with me? Why do I always feel like an outsider?

Before I could let the negative thoughts take me too far down the rabbit hole, I sat up as straight as I could and looked Drew squarely in the eye. I held up my red Solo cup as a toast.

"Tomorrow, Drew Laniere. Fifth period!"

* * *

It was 1:58. Fifth period had just begun, but no sign of Drew. I looked down the hallway in both directions and then pretended to look for something in my purse, in an effort to look nonchalant.

"Psst! Emme!" Drew's stage whisper emanated from a crack in the door to the boys' locker room. I squinted and could make out half of his face. "C'mon! Before anyone sees us!"

I squeezed through the heavy, half-open door to the boys' locker room, which had the faint smell of body odor mixed with soap, deodorant, and Polo cologne. Drew motioned to a communal bench in the center of one of the locker bays. I sat down and pulled out the bottle of Absolut I had absconded with from the family bar just hours before.

Drew held his hands up. "How are we drinking this?"

I grinned. "Don't worry. I thought of everything!" Then I dug two shot glasses out of my backpack.

Drew slapped me on the back as if I were one of the guys—although I noticed his hand lingered around my bra strap before he pulled it away. "You're awesome, Emme. Really cool."

I let his words of affirmation wash over me, even though I reminded myself that Drew was paying me a compliment only because I was his ticket to free alcohol.

He poured the clear liquid into each glass and handed me my vacation-themed shot glass that read "Virginia Is for Lovers." He held out his matching glass to mine, and we clinked them together before tilting our heads back. I could feel the vodka burn as it traveled down my throat. But before I could take too much notice, Drew was already pouring a second round. I ignored the sounds of footsteps outside the locker room as I downed the second—and then third—hastily poured shot. I also ignored Drew's free hand on my leg and his face moving closer to mine.

Instead of overthinking, I leaned in. Drew pressed his lips onto mine as his hand moved up my leg.

"Emme," he began. "I've always wanted to tell you this—"

"Hello?" The deep baritone voice, which definitely did *not* come from a student, interrupted whatever Drew was going to say next.

He put his hand over my lips, as if I needed someone to tell me not to make a noise.

"Is there someone in here?" the voice asked.

It was Coach Barnaby. His Southern drawl gave away his identity amidst the other teachers' voices, which had more of a Philly twang.

I gripped my shot glass tightly, as if it would somehow prevent Coach Barnaby from seeing us. The squeak from his Nikes grew closer, and I cringed when I saw his large frame fill the entrance to the locker bay we were sitting in.

Shit.

* * *

I sat in silence on the drive home, with my mom periodically looking over her shoulder from the passenger seat. She would open up her mouth, ready to say something, but then would seem to think better, because she'd turn back around to look out the windshield at Route 30.

My father, on the other hand, seemed to be able to multitask by driving and reaming me at the same time with little effort.

"Emme, what the hell were you thinking? You have no idea how lucky you are that Drew's parents brought in their lawyer. Because I sure as hell can't afford legal counsel for a daughter who had the hairbrained idea to drink at school! Seriously, what were you thinking?"

With my dad, it was never clear if his questions warranted an answer or if they were merely rhetorical, intended to make me feel remorse or think about how to change my ways. Deciding this question was the stew-in-your-juices variety, I remained mute.

What the hell was I doing? I know I want to be popular— to fit in—but why? For kids who only care about what I can do for them? For people I have nothing in common with? For some random guy I hope will consider me "cool" and "awesome"? Drew and his friends aren't going to care if I'm grounded forever and can't ride in the next show. The girls at the next show will be thrilled if I'm not there anyway. But I need the points for the finals! Ugh! I'm such an idiot.

At that moment, something shifted inside as I felt a memory . . .

I didn't remember it in my brain but instead felt the emotions of the first time I rode a pony. I couldn't have been more than four years old, but I remembered feeling like the most powerful person in the world as I held those reins. It was as if the pony and I were able to communicate wordlessly, and even in my preschool mind, I knew I had a talent with horses that was uncommon for others. Even when the woman from the backyard lesson barn praised my parents for my innate abilities, I wasn't buoyed by her words because this was one area where I didn't need affirmation. I felt accomplished inside. Comfortable.

The day I rode that stubborn little lesson pony, I knew I was enough. Good enough without having to do a thing except enjoy the feeling of riding that horse.

When did I lose that belief in myself?

Maybe it was the unbearable pressure to fit in, whether in the elitist horse show world or the cliques at school. Or maybe it was just the general unspoken rule that girls should be people-pleasers who are popular with boys, pretty, and only into hair, makeup, and clothes. And so smart that Ivy League colleges feel like the only option. But I wasn't that kind of girl—and never wanted to be. I wanted to be outside working. Just riding horses.

As my dad maneuvered our station wagon into the driveway, I made a pact with myself: *Emme, when the grounding of a lifetime that your dad promised is over, you're done with partying and trying to be the popular girl. You'll spend your time where it really matters—at the barn, with the horses. That's where you fit in. That's where you belong.*

CHAPTER 8

WILL WE SURVIVE?

OCTOBER 22, 2020

9:30 AM

I let out a deep sigh as I finished feeding the horses in their new "safe" pasture. What would normally be an effortless task had been nearly impossible, considering how hard the wind was blowing. At one point, I thought I was going to get blown off the feed wagon. Maybe it was the ominous wind, or maybe it was just having time to think as I went through the automatic motions of feeding the horses. Whatever the cause, I couldn't shake the paranoid feeling that the horses were not safe after the inferno we'd witnessed the night before.

"How goes it, Emme?" Hattie asked.

"Pretty good . . . I guess. I just can't ignore the feeling I have that we're not as safe as everyone thinks." I stared out at the field. "Look! Even the horses seem to know something is off."

We both watched as the horses furiously ran around the pasture—not a typical behavior for them. The fall yellows of the grass stood in stark contrast against a sky that was dark as night.

Hattie smiled with her classic look of wisdom. "I'm nervous too. But whatever nature throws our way, we'll handle it. I wouldn't be the fifth generation on this ranch if we weren't hearty folk. Besides, a good burn every few decades is great for the soil."

I smiled back, grateful for her sage words, as she continued. "And you see those American flags? They help monitor the wind. As long as they stay blowing in that there northeast direction, we're good."

I nodded, noting how the flags whipped in the same direction, like soldiers marching in tandem. Just beyond the flags, I caught a glimpse of Jessica and Molly roughhousing and flirting with the Smith cowboys.

She's right. Look at how relaxed everyone else is! Maybe the horses are running around to get a sense of their new digs. Maybe . . .

A gust of wind tore across the ranch, and, without thinking, I gazed at the flags. To my horror, they began turning in a southerly direction. Instead of flapping toward the northeast, they now pointed in the direction of what we kept calling the "safe" pasture.

Hattie coughed in response to the menacing wind change, which neither of us could ignore. But for once, instead of succumbing to my feelings of panic, I snapped into action mode.

"Excuse me," I began. "But I need to call ranch management."

The matriarch nodded and stepped aside as I walked into the farmhouse. Then I plopped into a kitchen chair and flipped open my laptop as I dialed the general manager's number.

"Jack? We need to call an emergency meeting."

Within five minutes, we were all on Zoom: Tom, Jack, the ranch owners, a few other members of the ranch leadership team, and me.

"Gentlemen, maybe I'm being overly dramatic," I said, "but the winds are insane—and the direction just shifted to the south, where the horses are located."

I watched the Brady Bunch-like squares on the screen reflect the same expressions of surprise and horror that I was sure I'd worn on my face moments earlier. But before I needed to make my case, Jack unmuted his microphone.

"Team, I agree with Emme. Nobody can figure out this fire—not even the experts! This fire is doing whatever it wants. Hell, it's creating its own damn weather." The other faces in the squares nodded in agreement.

I sat frozen in disbelief. Here I was, on a call with some of the most knowledgeable ranchers in the county, and they were falling silent and looking to me, the East Coast transplant, for guidance.

They must have noticed a change in my confidence since the first evacuation. It's like they're finally taking me seriously. As if they finally understand my purpose—and my commitment to their precious ranch and horses.

Despite the fear that welled up inside me once again, I squelched the feeling and said, "Thank you for that vote of confidence. With that said, it's time to evacuate . . . again. Even though the mandatory evacuation order hasn't gone into effect, it's just a matter of time."

Everyone agreed, and we made plans to touch base a few hours later.

The minute I hit the red End button to exit the meeting, my mind began spiraling. *Where can we go? Relocating two hundred horses is no easy feat!*

As if my prayers were being answered before I could even say them, my phone lit up. It was a text from Tom, letting me know that a ranch six miles down the road in Fraser, Colorado, had offered to take the horses.

It was tempting to text back a "Hell, yeah!" but in my heart, I knew that might still be too close to the fire. And if that were the case, we'd be looking at a third evacuation.

Slowly, I typed back a thanks-but-no-thanks text to the generous offer, madly trying to come up with other options. I remembered a friend of the ranch I had visited a few weeks before the fire. At the time, we were scoping out their property, Solid Rock Ranch, as a place to offer trail obstacles to our guests, from balance beams and teeter-totters to water features and pivot boxes. *Their place is perfect! And it's far enough away in Evergreen that the horses should be safe there.*

Within five minutes, I had gotten the okay from the Solid Rock ranch manager to evacuate the horses to their place. They had a hundred-and-fifty-acre pasture we could put the horses in. Not only did he immediately offer up his property, but he volunteered to help us get trailers together. I said a silent prayer of thanks that he was a member of the Roundup Riders of the Rockies—a group of more than two hundred cowboys who met every year for an epic ride. The Riders had been around since 1948, so I knew his connections would help immensely in soliciting volunteers.

Next, it was time to turn to my A-1 social media marketing team: the young C Lazy U wrangler girls. I texted the group what we needed, and almost instantly, I saw notifications popping up on my phone like popcorn: Instagram, Facebook, TikTok. Every social media app I had installed on my phone was blowing up!

I never thought I'd be glad those girls can't get off their phones. Their hobby is finally reaping rewards. And man, these kids are connected!

Before I knew what was happening, trailers began winding their way down the Smith driveway.

Help is here!

2:30 PM

What a difference a few hours makes!

Now that we were under mandatory evacuation orders—which, not surprisingly, were called soon after our Zoom meeting—the danger was palpable. This evacuation felt different from the last one; unlike before, I wasn't sure we had enough time to get the job done. Plus, we were at the mercy of volunteers who would need to be willing to drive in from all over the state, in the middle of a raging wildfire, to offer their assistance. The uncertainty of not knowing if an adequate number of trailers would show up was enough to make me feel like I was losing my mind.

As the first person on-site at the pasture, I immediately started haltering the horses. The situation felt deadly, as the flames licked the mountain ridge to the north. Time seemed to stand still as I waited for that first trailer to arrive.

After what felt like eons, I saw the headlights of trailer number one as it made its way toward me. Even though we needed way more than one trailer, this little ray of hope buoyed my spirits—and boy, did I need a lift at that moment. It was one of the Roundup Riders with a six-horse gooseneck.

He assured us that ten more trailers with Roundup Rider volunteers were a few minutes behind him and that we should not to worry.

I could see the land surrounding the C Lazy U in flames, off in the distance, as I watched from my "safe" front-row seat. I fought back tears as I witnessed propane tanks exploding and what looked like people's homes burning to the ground. It was a surreal scene that almost looked fake. Million-dollar homes collapsed like houses of cards, even though I knew some of the structures were incredibly well-built.

Nothing seems to be able to stand up to this fire.

I knew it would only be a matter of the wind shifting again, and the spot where I was standing could suddenly become a target for the flames that were taking no prisoners.

To distract myself from worrying about when the other trailers would arrive, I forced myself to consider our options. I hopped on a four-wheeler and drove toward the back of the pasture.

Okay, Plan B: cut the fence, spray-paint my number on the horses, and hope they outrun the fire.

Although I hated Plan B, Tom had made me promise earlier that if things got any worse, this would be the only option. While I knew he had my—and the staff's—best interests at heart, I couldn't stop the fear from welling up inside me.

I just can't leave those horses to burn. I may not have a choice, though.

But Tom had been insistent the night we'd discussed Plan B.

"Emme, get real. I love the horses, but I can't risk you putting your life in jeopardy. You need to remember your team too—and that would be putting them in a deadly situation. Think about how their parents would feel if we didn't take *their* safety into account."

Tom's voice had trailed off, insinuating what I knew was a distinct possibility. *If I wasn't willing to implement Plan B, I might be the one who would need to tell the family of one of my wranglers that their child was killed in the fire.*

"Okay," I had replied with resignation. "I'll do it. But only if there's a *mandate* that we need to get out fast. If it's just a recommendation, forget it."

That was enough of a capitulation for Tom, and he'd squeezed my hand. "Thanks, babe. Hopefully, we don't ever need to use Plan B."

Pulling out all the stops, I dialed Russell's number again. Thankfully, he picked up immediately and assured me he was already in his truck and on his way to assist. Within what seemed like seconds, he was rolling down the long road to the "safe" pasture in the back of the Smith ranch. Just his presence made me feel like we might, just might, have a chance of pulling this thing off.

3:30 PM

"Who should I load first?"

The innocuous question from the volunteer stopped me in my tracks, and it hit me: *Emme, you're deciding who lives and who dies.*

To prevent myself from losing my shit right then and there, I grabbed close to a dozen halters and walked toward Trigger, Fred, and Dually, who were grazing at the far end of the pasture. These three were my heart horses. While I tried not to have favorites, this trio stole my heart.

Without saying a word, Trigger walked toward me as if to say hello. I haltered him and buried my face in his neck, screaming and crying simultaneously. I knew I needed to pull it together—and fast. I couldn't let my team see me so upset.

The team can't see me like this! But I can't lose these horses. Not a single one of them.

Fortunately, within the next few hours, the ranching and equestrian community stepped up their game, showing up with anything, including fancy dressage and $300,000 polo rigs, cattle rigs with ramps, freight liners, six- to eighteen-horse trailers, and stock and open-top trailers. You name it, they were there!

Meanwhile, pasture communication was frantic, between terrible cell service and dropped location pins. We wanted to make it as easy as possible for the trailers to find us, but if someone was unfamiliar with the area, it was easy to drive by the dirt road that led to the pasture. To make matters worse, some rescuers thought the horses were still at the C Lazy U and found themselves in the thick smoke in Granby, ultimately forced to turn around.

But thank God for my girls! They were working their asses off, some holding more than ten horses at a time while the rest ran around, trying to catch and halter whoever they could. This chaotic yet seamless operation was working better than any of us could have ever imagined. Now we just had to pray that enough trailers would show up in time to get the horses out of there before the wind shifted again and the fire took out our pasture.

Kyra screamed, and I froze for a moment at the screeching sound before rushing over to her side. "What is it?"

As if a switch flipped on her emotions, Kyra was smiling.

"Never mind!" she said. "I thought we didn't have enough halters, but thanks to Allison's post, we've got enough coming in that we could halter every horse in Colorado if we wanted to!"

Inwardly, I smiled at Allison's transformation from being my disgruntled, passive-aggressive nemesis to working as a team member—and actually treating me with respect. Within the past few days, her steely exterior had seemed to melt away, replaced by a gritty, hard-working woman.

That version of her must have been there all along, just lurking beneath the surface. What's more, she didn't bristle at my recommendations anymore. Similar to those on the Zoom call, Allison appeared to respect my leadership. *Maybe she's stopped holding a grudge against me . . . finally!* I was grateful for all her experience with fires from growing up in Wyoming, and I was blessed to have her by my side.

That's when I realized that, like Allison, I might have had more resilience than I initially thought. Sure, I was sleep deprived, ravenously hungry, and stressed out beyond belief, but I was putting one foot in front of the other, getting things done, making difficult decisions—and keeping everyone alive.

Kyra yelled over, interrupting my thoughts. "Hey, Emme! Where are we headed with all these trailers?"

I laughed. Everyone was taking orders without even questioning where we were going to go once the horses were loaded. *That's progress! A few weeks ago, if I had asked one of them to do the tiniest favor, they would have grilled me to know why they needed to be inconvenienced.*

"We're going to travel over Berthoud Pass to Evergreen. It's about an hour and a half away. Not close, but it'll get everyone out of harm's way. We're heading to Solid Rock Ranch, our sanctuary ranch. You can google the address."

Kyra nodded and ran back to the group to relay the message—and I said a prayer that this move *would* keep us out of harm's way.

8:00 PM

As I watched one of the rescue trailers head toward Berthoud Pass, dozens of empty horse trailers continued to work their way toward the Smith ranch to save more horses. The rescuers shared nods as they passed one another as if to acknowledge the good deed they were doing that day.

Tom and his team continued directing traffic and keeping an eye on the fire. His eyes were bloodshot from sleep deprivation and worry, yet he shook hands and thanked each volunteer with gusto. The local police blocked traffic, and a long line formed because only a few trailers could enter the pasture at a time, as they needed plenty of room to turn around and exit after loading the horses.

Despite the political divisiveness our country had experienced that past year, it was reassuring to see this display of humanity: volunteers from all different backgrounds, cultures, and belief systems, all congregating to save two hundred horses they didn't know while working with people they'd never met.

The horses were just as incredible, allowing themselves to be loaded into trailers with complete strangers. By this point, there were only about forty horses left to load, and they were the more resistant ones—like Storm, who was so scared to trust these strange people. *When this is all over, I need to spend more time with her to rebuild that trust.*

Fortunately, one of the last rigs to show up was a luxury

polo rig, cleaned and waxed to the nines, with beautiful lights, spacious stalls, padded dividers, and shavings on the floor to pad the horses' feet. This was a far cry from some of the stock and cattle trailers the more cooperative horses had been loaded on.

I muttered under my breath, "Storm, it's your lucky day! Look at your ride."

But before I could enjoy the feeling of accomplishment in watching Storm give up the fight and allow herself to be loaded onto the extravagant vehicle, I noticed one of the Smith cowboys struggling with Waylon.

Waylon, one of our fastest horses, was white-eyed and scared. Despite being old, he would be impossible to catch if he made a run for it.

I felt like whatever strength I had in reserve to hold it together escaped me. I knew we were almost at the end of the evacuation, but Waylon's and Storm's reluctance had gotten to me. I took in the scene before me: dozens of recalcitrant horses that still needed to be loaded against a dark sky filled with so much smoke that we could barely see our hands in front of us. And now, as if the horses could sense that our patience had worn thin, some began running around in panic.

Unable to hold back my emotions and feeling like I might hyperventilate, I cursed and screamed, "Damn you, Waylon! Cooperate!" as I grabbed the reins from the frustrated cowboy. Even as the words flew out of my mouth, I knew full well this was exactly the opposite of what Waylon needed from me in that moment. Despite having Waylon under control, I knew that could change in an instant – especially if the horse connected with my own nervous energy and decided to go rogue again.

Fortunately, right then, one volunteer emerged from the chaos that was threatening to ruin our successful evacuation and walked over to me. The twentysomething polo player from Aspen was young, but he exuded confidence and calm that transcended his years.

"Ms. Emme, let me help out, okay? And you just hang in there. It's gonna be okay."

Without a word, I nodded and handed Waylon over to him. I lowered myself to the ground and took a few deep breaths as I watched him slowly pet Waylon on the neck. He picked up Waylon's rope, did some groundwork with him to get control of his feet, and slowly coaxed him into the trailer. As if the horse realized who was in charge, Waylon allowed himself to be led to the trailer without any fight or reluctance, happy to have a confident leader.

I collected myself and walked over to the volunteer with the polo rig. Storm was still making it difficult on them, but I could tell she was softening. I picked up her rope and followed the volunteer's lead; within a few minutes, Storm had allowed herself to be led onto the trailer.

As the wave of panic passed, I began to feel steadier. I stood up and walked over to the volunteer. "Hey," I started.

"Sorry about that meltdown. That's not me. I'm just so overwhelmed and tired. I freaked out because, y'know, we have no idea what's going to happen. I mean, are the horses even going to make it to where they're supposed to go?"

The volunteer smiled and won me over with his logic. "Ms. Emme, there are hundreds of trailers being escorted by police to safety. And the police aren't letting anyone out of their sight! I think they're going to figure out where to go."

Between his reasoning and gentle kindness, I was able to refocus. Most of the girls were back to their old selves too. In fact, I caught a few smiles from them.

Wow! Despite this madness, they still have it in them to smile. Amazing.

As we loaded the last group of horses onto the last volunteer's trailer, a tired and somewhat pathetic cheer rose from the group.

We did it! All the horses are on their way to safety. While the fire is still burning all around us, the horses are going to be okay. Now we just need to continue to pray that C Lazy U will make it.

As I walked back to my truck, I pulled my phone from my pocket and noticed the hundreds of missed texts and calls from volunteers.

But one text stood out in its menacing simplicity: *Ice storm.*

1:00 AM

Tom sat next to me on the hard couch in our hotel room, his hair still wet from the shower he had taken a few minutes earlier. I had wanted to drive to Solid Rock Ranch to make sure everyone made it safely, but cooler heads had prevailed.

"Emme, you're not going to be able to do anything tonight," Tom had said when he was convincing me not to go. "And to be honest, you'll be worth more to those horses if you get some sleep tonight and are ready to help out tomorrow morning."

I'd known he was right, so I had reluctantly agreed to spend the night with him in a hotel room in Winter Park after we finished loading the horses. But sleep was elusive, and I was still sitting upright on the couch when Tom emerged from the bathroom.

We were still getting calls, and apparently, while we had been busy fighting wind, fire, and dry conditions, the weather in Clear Creek County (on the other side of Berthoud Pass) had changed dramatically. They were experiencing an ice storm, and some of the trailers that had left the evacuation pasture well after dark and made it to the other side of the mountain pass had encountered that storm. The driving conditions were so treacherous that the trailers had to move at a snail's pace for fear of sliding off the slippery pass.

The driver of the polo rig—the one I affectionately called "Storm's Rig"—called Tom, who put the man on speakerphone.

"I'm okay, but man, it's nasty out here!" I could hear the sleet pelting the windshield, and I shivered. "Visibility is almost impossible, so I'm driving about five miles per hour, if that. Trucks and trailers are spinning out, and some even jackknifed and were pulled over on the side of I-70."

I envisioned Berthoud Pass, which had poor visibility on a good day, with its curves and steep drop-offs on either side.

"Where are you now?" Tom asked.

"I'm at the top of Floyd Hill," he answered. Floyd Hill was an unofficial point on I-70, where the mountains end and the foothills began. "But police are blocking the road and sending us on a detour. The good news is that the fog seems to be breaking. The detour will get the rest of us there, no problem."

Tom hung up, only to pick up again minutes later. The polo trailer had made it safely to Solid Rock Ranch.

"Tom, the scene here is crazy. There's no drop-off point because it's too narrow to drive the horses into the actual pasture. So they have a bunch of Roundup Riders here unloading the horses and walking them about a quarter mile to their new pasture. And the horses in the pasture are running around a bit, yelling for their friends."

Tom replied, "That's exactly what they'd be doing. But other than being disoriented, are they okay?"

"They seem to be! I won't lie, though. Some of them are slipping and sliding on their walk. It's just so icy! But it looks like they're all just fine, from what I can see anyway. It's pitch black out here and snowing and sleeting hard. Thank God Storm made it just fine! The volunteers are walking her to the pasture now."

Tom smiled.

"That's my Storm!" I yelled from across the room, hoping the driver could hear me. He must have, because he said, "Is that your wife?"

"Sure is!" Tom said. "She's one helluva lady—and those horses wouldn't be where they are now if it weren't for her and volunteers like you! I can't thank you enough for what you did tonight."

Knowing the horses were finally safe, I allowed Tom to take my hand and lead me into the bedroom. We collapsed on the bed, and he flicked the remote. The map of Colorado lit the screen as the meteorologist pointed at the graphics that depicted the fire damage. Tom kept the television on mute, and we watched the screen, depleted yet grateful to be in a warm bed.

As my eyes closed, I felt Tom's phone vibrate. He slid the button and said, "Hey, Jack. Everything okay?" I watched his smile turn grim. He hung up the phone.

"What is it?"

Tom turned to face me. "Emme, the barn burned, and C Lazy U is on fire."

Hearing his words, I rolled over, tears of grief streaming down my face. I stopped trying to pretend I was okay as I let myself wail and sob. Tom put his arm around my waist and pulled me close to him. Even though he wasn't hysterically crying like I was, I knew he felt the same way. I knew we both were wondering the same thing: *Will the ranch survive? Will we have jobs? Will the horses have a home to return to?*

SIX MONTHS BEFORE THE FIRE
APRIL 2020

Your father passed away last night.

The flight attendant motioned to the exit signs as part of her preflight spiel, but all I could hear were my mother's words reverberating in my head like a bad song stuck on repeat. Ever since that fateful phone call less than a day earlier, her words had occupied my thoughts, except when I was at work. At the ranch, I got a reprieve from those thoughts, between caring for the horses and the guests, who had been unusually demanding recently due to the COVID scare.

But now, on this 737 bound from Denver to Philadelphia, all I could hear was the conversation between my mother and me. Healthy as a horse himself, my father was the last person I would have expected to fall victim to a heart attack. A healthy eater and moderate drinker who worked out daily, he had been the poster child for a senior living his best life.

The day it happened, I had finished sweeping the barn and

was looking forward to dinner out with Tom as I drove home. We were celebrating our anniversary a few weeks late, and I had promised him I wouldn't stay late at C Lazy U—for once. I was humming along to a Ryan Bingham song on the radio when my mom's name popped up on my phone. Figuring she wanted to wish us a happy belated anniversary celebration— or maybe remind me yet again to call the fertility doctor she had seen on *The Doctors* who happened to practice in Denver—I thought nothing of picking up while driving. No sooner had the words come out of her mouth than I found myself pulling over in the parking lot of a convenience store, practically hyperventilating.

Dead? Dad?

And now, less than twenty-four hours later, there I was, with Tom by my side, headed to my childhood home . . . and the funeral home. As the plane taxied down the runway, I attempted to drown out my thoughts with the airline-issued headset. No matter how much I tried to focus on the in-flight movie or lose myself in the Southwest Airlines radio station, the flood of memories haunted me—especially that day at the barn. It was a day I would never forget, and even though it was so many years ago, it felt like yesterday . . .

It had been shortly after the Drew debacle, and I needed to blow off steam and process what had happened. I had decided to take Gracie out on a trail ride. As my junior hunter, Gracie wasn't all that great of a trail horse and could be a giant spook outside the arena, but I really didn't care at that moment. As I hacked her around the pastures, I remained lost in thought about how stupid I'd been to let Drew take advantage of me that way. Between the dense fog and being so deep in thought, I didn't notice when the ground changed and Gracie's hoof sunk into a thick mud puddle. Without the ability to move her feet, she'd panicked, jumping around and bucking as she tried to free herself from the mud. That's when I lost my balance and was catapulted off the saddle headfirst into the mud just inches from a tree. More shaken than injured and covered in head-to-toe mud, I watched Gracie gallop back to the stable, riderless.

Shit.

I walked the mile or so back to the stable and called my dad. Being grounded meant I'd lost car privileges for the next month, so Dad had been driving me to and from the barn each day.

When he pulled up, he immediately noticed my ripped breeches and muddy shirt and boots. "You okay, honey?" he asked.

I got in the car, and as we pulled out of the driveway, I nodded, trying not to cry—but failing—so I explained what happened with Gracie.

"But we're both okay," I said. Frustrated, I sighed. "I guess this is just another run of bad luck for me. First at school with Drew, and now with the horses."

Without a word, my dad made a sudden right turn and pulled into the Wawa parking lot. "What kind of hoagie?"

I gave him a weak smile. "Italian, please. Extra mayo."

A few minutes later, he emerged with two sandwiches. We sat silently for a few minutes in the parking lot, eating, before he spoke.

"Emme, what happened today isn't bad luck. You were distracted because of what happened at school with that Drew kid, and you weren't your typical conscientious self. Luckily, you and Gracie are just fine, so that's where you can count yourself lucky. But don't think everything is stacked against you."

I locked eyes with my father, not knowing where he was going with the conversation.

He continued. "I was pretty hot about getting the call to pick you up at school for drinking, but I've had some time to think about it, and I have a theory."

I was smart enough to know that, even though my dad was a quiet man, when he had a theory, there were going to be some sage words headed my way. He was kind of like that guy from the ads: "When E. F. Hutton talks, people *listen.*"

My dad looked out the windshield as if God was giving him the words to say next. "Emme, you're gifted. And you're wise. And you're growing into a fantastic rider and strong woman. Animals respond to you in a way that is nothing short of amazing. To be honest, I think your old-soul nature sometimes makes you feel like an outsider with your peers."

I nodded in agreement. *How does he know that?*

"So," he continued, "when you have a gift *and* you're smart, people can't always relate. Some are jealous, and others just don't get you. But that doesn't mean there's anything wrong with you. In fact, it's just the opposite: you have abilities and instincts that are going to take you far in life. You have the potential to be a true leader based on merit—and not just someone who wins popularity contests. The only problem, as I see it, is that you don't realize your worth. So you sometimes sell out to fit in."

As his words sunk in, I finally felt like someone understood me. *Maybe my dad was like that as a kid too!* But rather than ask questions to learn more about what gave him these insights, I simply blushed and said, "Thanks, Dad."

From that day forward, I felt gratitude toward my father for helping me see something special in myself. Even though I didn't completely understand what exactly he was seeing at the time, I trusted that he might know more than I did as a teenager.

After that talk, no matter how low I felt, I would replay that conversation in the Wawa parking lot in my head to buoy my spirits. I thought about his words the day I decided to go to C Lazy U with Laura for the first time. The day I took the bar. The day I exploded at Reed. And the day I decided to leave law.

Now, as I looked out the window at the puffy clouds, I tried to figure out how to roll those memories—and an overdue thank-you to my father—into an eloquent eulogy.

My mom was way too much of a basket case at the moment to pull a speech together, so when she asked me to do the honors, I immediately agreed. I started scribbling some initial ideas on the napkin the flight attendant handed me with my Diet Coke, but I couldn't seem to capture the depth of feeling in words.

The man in the seat next to me took notice of my frustration. "Writer's block?" he asked.

I smiled through the tears that welled up in my eyes and nodded. "Yeah. For my dad's funeral."

The man exhaled slowly. "I'm sorry for your loss—and I get it. My dad passed away last year, and I was the only one who stepped up to make the speech. You'd think in a family of eight, someone else would have offered, but everyone's always happy to leave it to the oldest to take care of things." His laugh was tinged with the deep sorrow that only someone who'd lost a parent understands.

I met his eyes and returned his sad smile with my own. "I'm an only, so I'm the oldest, the middle, and the baby. Lucky me." I paused. "So, tell me, how did you know what to say? I feel like I don't do it justice when I try to summarize a life in just a few words. I mean, he was so wise. And he was the first person to see positive things in me that I couldn't see in myself. I'm so grateful."

Now the man gave a genuine laugh. "Hell, you've got a definite advantage! When it came to my dad, here's the material I had to work with: if he wasn't drunk, sleeping around, or checked out because he was 'too depressed' and 'struggling,' he was an okay dad. At least your dad sounds like a stand-up guy."

His words hit me. Even in the depths of my own despair, I couldn't imagine a father like this man described.

"You're 100 percent right," I said. "He was an incredible person. Not perfect, of course, but I couldn't have asked for anyone better. He always supported me and encouraged me to do whatever made me happy."

The man smiled. "Then say that! Everything you told me is perfect. And I'm sure all of it would make your dad proud."

The flight attendant returned to our row, asking if we wanted anything else. I held up my credit card. "Three shots of bourbon—one for me, one for my husband, and one for—" I looked at the man. "Sorry, what's your name?"

"Mike."

That single syllable took my breath away. I turned toward Tom, and we locked eyes in amazement. Mike was my father's name.

As Mike and I did our best to clink plastic cups together in memory of our dads, I closed my eyes. *I never believed in the afterlife before. But, Dad, if Mike is your sign to me that you approve of my speech, then thank you! Thank you for who you were—and who you are. The words you said to me all those years ago have helped me more than you know. I think that no matter what life hands me, nothing will be more than*

I can handle. No emergency. No crisis. Hell, not even losing you will be too much for me—and that is thanks to you.

After some polite small talk with Mike, I closed my eyes and snuggled up on Tom's shoulder to catch a nap. As I drifted off to sleep, I saw my father in my mind's eye, smiling and proud.

AFTER THE FIRE
OCTOBER 23, 2020
10:00 AM

As the snow blanketed the ground in Evergreen, I sat at the kitchen table in the small Solid Rock Ranch guest house where I was staying, coffee mug in hand. I'd given up another IVF appointment, was sacrificing time with Tom, and had decided to stay in Evergreen so I could care for the herd until we knew what would happen next. Although I missed my husband, I was enjoying the quiet and peaceful sanctuary, well away from any signs of fire or danger.

Relieved that the horses were safe and enjoying their temporary new home, I felt emotionally stable enough to run a Google search on the fire—knowing that not everyone had fared so well.

The reporters provided detailed accounts of the East Troublesome Fire, declaring it one of the most destructive fires in Colorado history. The formal damage assessments reported that two hundred thousand acres—about the area of San Antonio, Texas—had been scorched in northern Grand County. That was approximately 15 percent of the county.

Blotting my eyes with a tissue, I continued reading: "The burn scar over public land spans from the Bureau of Land Management to U.S. Forest Service land and Rocky Mountain National Park. In total, 555 structures suffered damage, including 366 residential buildings and 189 outbuildings. Perhaps most tragic, more than 200 of the homes lost were reported as primary residences."

I put the paper down and looked out the window as Tom pulled up the long driveway. He was holding down the fort back home and at C Lazy U. We Skyped in the evenings while we ate dinner to reconnect and fill one another in on the progress at the ranch and the status of the horses. Bracing myself for him to share what things looked like there, I sat up straight and held my breath.

Tom walked through the front door, rays of sunlight streaming into the hallway and illuminating his unshaven face. He approached the table and held out his hand. I took it and squeezed with all my might.

"So?"

He smiled, and I recognized this expression as the one he used to soften any bad news he needed to share. "Thank God, everyone is safe," he said.

The tears began to flow, and I sputtered, "That doesn't sound good at all! How bad is it?"

I learned that the ranch had lost eight members' homes, two staff housing units, a guest cabin, the hay shed—including thousands of tons of hay—and the historic barn.

"There's lots of scorched land, and the pasture and fence lines have been destroyed. The corrals burned, and pretty much every building has been damaged in some way or another. I'm pretty sure some of the cabins that are standing are still going to need an entire renovation from the smoke damage. But, hon—"

I locked eyes with Tom, knowing this was the part where he would try to cheer me up.

"Let's remember that everyone is safe. And compared to all those other families who lost their homes, we still have ours. Even the ranch fared well in comparison to so many other people's homes and property. The fire stopped short of the Smith ranch, so they were lucky too."

As Tom's words sunk in, I realized he was right. *We could be grieving the loss of lives—staff and the horses. But we're not. It's a business disaster for sure, and the damage sounds catastrophic. But those are all things—and things can be repaired, while lost lives cannot.*

We really are *fortunate.*

OCTOBER 25, 2020

Snow continued to fall on the burned landscape of C Lazy U, and the desperately needed moisture helped decrease the threat of more fire damage. As we continued to learn more, we found out that many ranches in Grand County, including the C Lazy U, reported a significant or total loss of hay, which had been intended for the livestock's winter feeding. Various watersheds hit by the fire included Willow Creek, which runs directly through the C Lazy U and was the primary source of water for the horses. According to the county commissioner, it was possible that sedimentation, debris flows, and water contamination would threaten drinking water for years to come.

"Next week," Tom said over the spicy farmhouse burgers and fries he had picked up from Debbie's Drive-In on the way home, "the horses might be able to return home."

I took a big gulp of beer, and I finally felt a spark of genuine happiness—the first time I'd felt that way since the fire started. "That's the best news I've heard in weeks!"

Tom smiled and looked deep into my eyes. "I've missed you, Emme. We did what we had to do, but it's time to come home."

I giggled. "I know. Although I love horses, Storm isn't the best sleeping buddy. I've missed you too. It's time for *everyone* to return home."

He grinned as I raised my eyebrows with a knowing

look. Tom understood full well what I meant: I wouldn't leave Solid Rock Ranch until every last horse was back at C Lazy U.

NOVEMBER 12, 2020
7:00 AM

Thanks to the many volunteers' love for the horses, we were able to successfully transport all of the horses back to the ranch. Now that they had returned home, I walked the grounds of C Lazy U, surveying the damage for the first time.

Despite everything being covered in snow, I gasped as I took in the destruction: the historic barn was now a pile of burned ash, and the scorched hay was still smoldering. Fortunately, many of our fellow dude ranchers had promised to donate hay and feed. The outpouring of generosity and support from the equine community continued to render me speechless, knowing that the horses would be comfortable and well-fed. Most importantly, they were back home, safe in West Meadow, which had been spared by the fire.

The return trip for the horses had been uneventful and smooth—the opposite experience of the frantic jingles during the evacuation. Even Storm had allowed herself to be loaded onto the trailer without incident.

Thinking of Storm, I smiled as I boarded the wagon to feed the horses. *That girl loves to eat! I'll bet she can't wait for me today.* The morning was crisp and cold, and all the horses were eager to get their breakfast. As we drove around the pasture, dropping hay, they chased the wagon and fought one another in an attempt to get closer to the piles. As they jockeyed for a better position, I heard a loud crack that took my breath away. It's the sound every horseman fears: the sound of breaking bone.

I looked up to see which horse was hurt, and there was Storm, hopping around on three legs. For a moment, she stopped moving and just stood there, trembling. I jumped off the wagon and ran over to her. Within seconds, I knew her leg was broken. I picked up my cell phone and called one of the hunting guides to assist. I knew what had to be done. And it broke my heart.

7:30 AM

I stood over Storm's body, bawling. My worst fears had been confirmed when the guide joined me: it was a compound fracture, and that meant we needed to do what I dreaded most: euthanize this young, vibrant horse. *This horse that has just survived the fire. That has overcome so much.*

Minutes after she passed, Tom raced out to the pasture and rushed to my side.

"Emme, I'm so sorry! I just heard." He looked at Storm with affection. "Poor girl. At least she died at home."

I shook my head and sniffled. "Yes, in the pasture with her herd mates. At least it didn't happen during the evacuation." But even this was little consolation for the devastation I felt.

Tom wrapped his arms around me as I began crying again. "Let's go for a walk. Check on the other horses," he suggested, and I allowed him to lead me away from Storm, if only for a few minutes.

As we checked on the horses, my phone rang with an unfamiliar number lighting up the screen. I wiped my eyes and swiped to accept the call.

"Hello?"

"Hi, Emme? This is Belinda Bradshaw. How are you?"

Belinda? I struggled to keep my voice steady. "To be honest, I'm not having the best day. We just lost one of our girls."

She gasped, "Ohmigod! Was it Molly? Or Lexi? Who?"

Despite my grief, I smiled. Most people didn't know how much these horses were like people to me.

"No, not one of those girls. Storm, one of our horses." I closed my eyes with reverence as I spoke Storm's name.

Belinda coughed, clearly uncomfortable. "Oh, okay. Um, I'm sorry one of your horses died."

I knew she was not attached to the horses at all and probably couldn't relate, but I couldn't be angry. Belinda Radshaw never was—and never would be—a horse person.

"Thank you," I said. "But I'm sure you called for a different reason."

Belinda recovered quickly, and her voice brightened. "Oh, yes! I've been thinking about what I could do to help. Of course, you know I'd be a hopeless mess doing any manual labor." She paused, and I tried to imagine Belinda cleaning out a smoke-ravaged guest house but couldn't picture it, even in my mind.

"Well, I did take some time last week to go through my wardrobe. Time to get rid of the outdated items, you know? So, I currently have about ten boxes' worth of clothing I'd like to donate to any of your displaced staff who may need it. And my husband and I would like to donate $50,000 to the ranch. We just need to know who to make the check payable to and where to deliver the clothing."

I stood in the pasture, speechless. For a moment, I put aside my thoughts about Storm to acknowledge the selflessness of this guest, who clearly cared not just about the ranch as a vacation spot but about the people who worked there.

"Oh my God, Belinda, thank you so much! You're amazing! I can tell you, on behalf of everyone at the ranch, your generosity is beyond measure. I can't even express my gratitude in words."

We hung up, and I imagined what the wranglers might look like in Belinda Radshaw's designer clothes. *Our wranglers are going to be runway ready!* Even with the loss of Storm, there was no denying that Belinda's call buoyed my spirits.

That bittersweet feeling remained with me all day long as I went through the motions: making the arrangements to remove Storm's body, checking on the other horses, and answering emails and calls from the staff. The deep sadness that comes from losing a horse mixed with gratitude as donation after donation continued to pour in. While the Radshaw gift was the largest, hundreds of people sent money, clothes, and supplies. One member even set up a GoFundMe campaign to raise more money for the staff and our ranch neighbors who had lost their homes.

Everyone was anxious for C Lazy U to return to operation again. The ranch had been around for a century, and we were going to do everything in our power to restore it so it could operate for another hundred years. To be honest, I felt as if the rebuilding effort was a fitting metaphorical fuck-you to Mother Nature that sent a clear message: C Lazy U might be down and out right now, but we would come together to repair and return—better than ever before!

C LAZY U: THE EARLY DAYS
MARCH 2012

The sun reflected off the freshly fallen snow, and everything around us sparkled. Tom and I were standing at the top of Mount Baldy, looking down at the horses happily munching on their hay in West Meadow, along with Russell, who'd graciously taken an online course to become a certified marriage officiant.

It was difficult to believe that Tom and I had connected a mere nine months before. But after my dysfunctional relationship with Reed, it took me little time to realize that Tom was different. In fact, I knew by the end of our second date—a picnic near Lake Granby—that Tom was the one.

I shivered, and Tom wrapped his parka around my bare shoulders. I had stubbornly insisted on wearing a strapless gown, if you'd call it that. It was more of a glamorous après-ski top. I'd fallen in love with its off-white simplicity and frivolity. The white faux fur shawl that I had bought to keep me warm was not even coming close to doing the trick. Despite eschewing a materialistic lifestyle track, I did occasionally enjoy treating myself to completely impractical things, and this strapless number epitomized that. At the same time, I couldn't wait to ski down to the lodge and bundle up in some sensible Gore-Tex.

Tom whispered in my ear. "I love you, Emme: your wit, your brain . . . everything! But most of all, your free spirit. I never thought I'd meet a soulmate—someone who could easily follow the path of what everyone else expected of us while knowing she wanted more out of life."

I hugged Tom back, my heart feeling so full it might explode. This moment couldn't have been more perfect: just me, Tom, and the mountain. No parents, no friends, and no expectations for the "perfect" wedding. Although I knew everyone would be a bit disappointed that we'd eloped, we made a promise to have a get-together back East to give everyone the big party they would appreciate. In our minds, it would be more like a reunion than a reception, but they could call it whatever they wanted! With this way, *our* way, we were able to experience an intimate exchange of vows that were truly meaningful.

Russell stumbled a bit over his words, but when he got to the final sentence, he could not have been clearer.

"By the power vested in me, by the State of Colorado, I now pronounce you husband and wife."

Tom and I kissed, and all I could think of was the old Frank Sinatra refrain.

I did it my way.

AUTHOR'S NOTE

This story began soon after the East Troublesome Fire ended. I started writing down everything I could remember about the fire, the events, and the people. Slowly, the story evolved from there. What began as a personal memoir as part of a massive effort to rescue two hundred dude ranch horses from a wildfire turned into a fictionalized version of events and people from my life, centered around this traumatic event. While this story is based on a true story, the characters themselves are fictionalized. (Although, I am sure those who know me can draw many similarities between Emme and me.) Likewise, some of the events have been embellished to keep the reader engaged. A wonderful network of creative minds and people gave me the courage to evolve the story into something more.

In writing this story, it was important for me to show the reader how vastly different my experience was with horses prior to C Lazy U. Before the ranch, horses were a childhood love of mine that turned into a sport—a sport I absolutely love, even to this day. Growing up in the hunter/jumper world taught me so much about myself and gave me direction. I knew from a very young age that I wanted horses to be a part of my life, and my vision never strayed from that. I always imagined I would live somewhere in the Northeast, work as an attorney, be married with kids, and show in the hunter/jumpers as an amateur on the weekends for fun. I always thought I would have a couple of nice hunters and possibly a big fancy jumper as well.

Ha! How wrong I was! Like many, the grunt of everyday life took over, and I found it harder and harder to prioritize horses. Making money to afford the horses also took over. I had no idea how to balance a career and horses while putting a roof over my head.

Horses began to feel like a gigantic financial burden—so much so that I began to not enjoy riding. I started to feel like an entirely different person. Maybe this was just a part of growing up, but it didn't make sense to me and just felt wrong. Luckily, the realization that my life was headed in a direction that I did not intend stopped me dead in my tracks. I needed to make a change, but I had no clue what that was until I found the ranch and fell in love with some dude horses.

I did not intend to leave my law career, never to return. For years, I doubted my decision to stay on at the ranch and always thought I had no choice but to return to law. Sure, it was incredibly difficult to walk away from a promising legal career I had worked so hard for. But whenever I thought about returning to law and leaving the ranch, I couldn't actually make myself do it. As the years passed, I became more at peace with my choice and finally accepted that this was my destiny. This was what made me happy. I needed to let go of what I thought I was *supposed* to do and accept the fact that an equine professional was who I was always meant to *be*.

Horses teach us to listen to our guts. They require us to have a relationship with them and be honest with ourselves. The saying "Horses are a mirror into our soul" couldn't be more true. My relationship with horses kept me true to myself and provided me with the courage to leave the predictability of what my life had become and guided me into something extraordinary.

There have been so many great horses that have taught me so much along the way. Most importantly, they have given me the confidence to follow my heart and allow the journey to happen. So, parents, when your child asks for a pony or a riding lesson, DO IT! The benefits of having these animals in your life far outweigh the expense. And there are so many ways to have horses in your life. It doesn't have to be a certain discipline, a certain way, or even one particular type of horse. Horses themselves are a lifelong journey— one on which you learn something new about them, other people, or yourself, time and time again. After all, without horses, this story would never have been created, nor would I have ever had the courage to lead a team of young wranglers in the rescue of over two hundred horses from one of the worst fires in Colorado's history.

C Lazy U Ranch is a wonderful place that is very near and dear to my heart. It's been the premier Colorado dude ranch for over a century. It is a sanctuary where guests leave the stresses of their everyday life behind and immerse themselves in the beauty of the land, the horses, and the world-class hospitality—if only for a short time. After all, playing cowboy for a week is a lot of fun!

For me, the ranch is a dude ranch vacation and a lifelong passion for horses turned into a career. It's a place that gave me direction and a purpose when I was navigating my way through young adulthood. Walking away from my law career and education to follow a thought I had on vacation was not an easy decision. It was also one you could easily argue was slightly demented. However, I have never looked back, because every step of this wild ride has been more gratifying than the last.

The friendships I have made and the people I have met at C Lazy U have been life-changing. I will be forever grateful to this wonderful ranch for welcoming me as part of its legacy and for giving me something I never dreamed possible. The East Troublesome Fire was just another part of the ranch's story, and I'm sure that the many people involved with the ranch all have their very own stories as well. I'm grateful you took the time to read mine.

Many thanks to the ranch ownership, members, guests, and team members who encouraged me along the way. The people who have worked there over the years have all played an integral part of creating this wonderful place. C Lazy U Ranch is just one of many wonderful ranches out West that offer their guests a reprieve from their everyday lives. I encourage you to work at a dude ranch if you ride horses and are passionate about learning as much as you can, whether you want a career with horses, a fun summer away from it all, or an excuse to spend time in the mountains. Or, just take your family or your best friend for a wonderful vacation far away from your everyday stresses. The experience could change your life too!

To learn more about the C Lazy U Ranch or other wonderful dude ranches, you can find more information here: www.clazyu.com, www.duderanch.org, www.coloradoranch.com.

ACKNOWLEDGMENTS

This book is dedicated to my extraordinary husband, for without him, this crazy journey would not be possible. Thank you for always believing in me and partnering with me to embrace uncertainty and venturing from the norm. I love you.

Thank you to my parents for *everything* and for introducing me to horses at a young age. Our family may be small, but it is mighty. I know Dad is smiling down on me: I wrote a book!

Thank you to the C Lazy U Ranch for being my sanctuary and my home away from home.

Lastly, thank you to all the horse girls who have been a part of my life. There are so many of you. Some I have gotten to know well; some I have admired from afar. Without your support, passion, and friendship, this crazy lifelong ride we are all on would not have been nearly as fun.

ABOUT THE AUTHOR

Ami Cullen hails from Chester County, Pennsylvania, where her love for horses first blossomed. Growing up, she competed in the hunter/jumper discipline at the national level. After earning her law degree from the Catholic University School of Law in Washington, D.C., Ami practiced medical malpractice defense law at a firm in Bethesda, Maryland.  However, it was during a vacation at the C Lazy U Ranch that she discovered her true passion—ranch life and taking care of horses.

Currently, Ami is the Director of Equestrian Operations and oversees all aspects of the C Lazy U Ranch's Equine Program. Certified as a Horsemanship Association Instructor in both English and Western disciplines, Ami delights in connecting people with horses and teaching novice equestrians' horsemanship.

Ami resides in Granby, Colorado, with her husband Mike, their cat, River, and their two dogs: Esther, a Blue Heeler, and

Arlo, a Jack Russell Terrier. Her journey from legal practice to ranch life is a testament to following one's heart and finding fulfillment in unexpected places.

Contact Ami at: Cullenami79@gmail.com.

26142346R00111